About this book

Simply put, this book is geared to readers who don't have a bunch of fancy tools or a lot of nuts 'n bolts experience. It's a book for busy people who don't have time for long, obscure explanations. And it's a book that tackles the most common car (and truck!) problems you're likely to meet up with.

Most of what you'll find here comes from the pages of THE FAMILY HANDYMAN magazine, which means that every word and illustration had to pass over the desk—or tool chest—of all sorts of nitpicky folks to begin with. Then we gathered up the best of our automotive material and scrutinized it all over again, adding important new information and some new illustrations. The result? A handy, hardworking book that explains the most common repairs, maintenance, and improvements from headlight to tailpipe.

Keep it in your library or glove compartment for ready reference, or give it to your kids when they first start to drive (and don't want to hear *you* lecture about car care!). No matter what kind of car you drive, you'll find this information timely and straightforward.

We've tried to make this book "driver-friendly," too, with a number of special features:

• Any words that you might not understand are **highlighted**; you'll find simple definitions of each in the glossary that starts on page 182.

• To complement all the do-it-yourself information, we've included a set of checklists that you can fill out and hand to your mechanic when you'd rather have someone else do the work. The checklists start on page 185 and will help the mechanic figure out what's *really* going on with your car, and that just might save you some money.

• Finally, we've stocked the pages with plenty of illustrations and some easy-to-understand charts.

The first issue of THE FAMILY HANDYMAN came out when the first Corvette rolled off the assembly line about 45 years ago. And as always, we'll continue to present do-it-yourself information in a clear, understandable *do*-able manner.

GARY HAVENS, EDITOR
The Family Handyman

Contents

THE FAMILY Handyman

Simple Car Care & Repair

THE READER'S DIGEST ASSOCIATION, INC.
PLEASANTVILLE, NEW YORK • MONTREAL

Reader's Digest Project Staff

Project Editor
Mark Feirer

Designer
Ronald Gross

Copyeditor
Kathie Ness

Contributing Editor
Bob Lacivita

Reader's Digest Illustrated Reference Books

Editor-in-Chief
Christopher Cavanaugh

Art Director
Joan Mazzeo

Operations Manager
William J. Cassidy

Director, Trade Publishing
Christopher T. Reggio

Senior Design Director
Elizabeth L. Tunnicliffe

Reader's Digest and the Pegasus logo are registered trademarks
of The Reader's Digest Association, Inc.

The Family Handyman is a registered trademark of RD Publications, Inc.
Printed in Peru
Fourth Printing, September 2003

The Family Handyman

Editor
Gary Havens

Managing Editor
Mark Thompson

Book Editor
Spike Carlsen

Consultants
Paul Brand, Dave Radtke, Mort Schultz, Mac Wentz

Editorial Assistant
Michaela Wentz

Illustrators
Ron Chamberlain, Don Mannes, Doug Oudekerk

Photography
Bill Zuehlke

Library of Congress Cataloging in Publication Data
The family handyman simple car care & repair
        p. cm.
   Includes index.
   ISBN 0-89577-930-7
    1. Automobiles–Maintenance and repair–Amateurs' manuals.
  I. Reader's Digest Association.   II. Family handyman.
  TL152.F329   1997
  629.28′72–dc21   96-47545

To order additional copies of *THE FAMILY HANDYMAN Simple Car Care & Repair,*
call 1-800-846-2100.

Visit us on our website at: www.rd.com.

Ready to Roll

Owning a car is a lot like owning a boat. Most days you're just going to sail along, enjoying the nice weather and the new experiences travel brings. Life is great, isn't it? Then there are the days when the wind howls, waves surge over the bow, and it's definitely sink-or-sail time. That's when you'll get the most satisfaction out of all those emergency preparations you made (didn't you?).

What you have to remember is that there's no perfect mechanical device. There's no guarantee, no matter how much money you paid for your car, that it will always be ready, willing, and able to take you anywhere. Sometimes car problems come with the weather, sometimes they come with another driver (ker-CRASH!). Some are seemingly minor annoyances that can grow into full-size problems if left untended. And all too often problems come when you least expect them and can least afford to fix them.

Playing it safe

Working safely on your car

Working on a car can be dangerous, but a cautious, well-informed mechanic (amateur or otherwise) needn't worry. Here are some things to keep in mind as you're working:

✔Remove rings, watches, and any other jewelry so they won't catch on obstructions.

✔Loose clothes and long hair can get caught in moving parts. Button cuffs, tuck in your shirt, and tie up your hair or tuck it under a cap.

✔Never work on any vehicle without having a suitable (rated A-B-C) dry-chemical **fire extinguisher** handy—a little money buys a lot of protection here.

✔Safety glasses or goggles are not optional. Wear them.

✔Exhaust is toxic, so try to work outdoors if the engine will be running. If you do the work indoors, run a hose (a shop-vacuum hose may fit) from the tailpipe of the car to the outside.

✔Sure, the top of the battery seems like a convenient tool tray, but it's a dangerous one! An accidental connection between the two terminals will shock or burn you, damage the battery and wiring, or even cause the battery to explode.

✔Always engage the parking brake, and put the **transmission** in *Park* (automatics) or *Neutral* (manual transmissions).

✔Don't smoke or have an open flame nearby: car work involves lots of flammable substances.

✔Anything connected to the engine, transmission, **differential**, or exhaust system could be hot. And never remove the **radiator** cap while the engine is still hot!

✔Work under a vehicle only if it's safely supported by either jack stands or drive-up ramps (see p. 24). Never use the factory-supplied jack for this purpose— it's only for changing tires. Set the parking brake, and use **wheel chocks** behind any wheels still on the ground.

✔Don't rush. Keep children and pets away. If you're working alone, arrange to have someone check on you periodically.

✔Gasoline is highly toxic, so never siphon fuel by mouth. **Antifreeze** is also toxic, and its sweet smell is enticing, making pets and children the likely poisoning victims.

✔A vehicle's ignition system packs a wallop—as much as 50,000 volts. While seldom lethal, a shock can cause you to jerk involuntarily and injure yourself. If you must touch ignition wires while the engine is running, use insulated pliers.

✔Watch the cooling fan! Modern electric fans can switch on at any time, even if the engine is shut off.

Unsafe safety belt

While you are driving on a curved entry ramp leading onto a highway, the shoulder belt of your vehicle may lock, preventing you from leaning forward to see oncoming traffic.

Most seat belt retractors are designed with an inertia-reel pendulum in the belt housing; it causes the belt to lock it in place when the vehicle is quickly decelerating, even during moderate braking or cornering.

Before you conclude that something's wrong with the mechanism, make sure it isn't twisted in the retractor or the belt guides. If problems continue but the dealership says this behavior is normal, try this: Try to do all your braking before getting onto the ramp, try not to lean forward, and if the belt still locks, lean back slightly to release the inertia reel. This should loosen the belt, and you'll be able to lean forward again so you can see better.

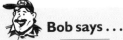

Bob says . . .

Checking seat belts after an accident

Seat belts are placed under tremendous stress during an accident, especially if the impact was serious enough to deploy the air bag. Your body shop and insurance adjuster should inspect the seat belt material around the areas of greatest stress: the guides, retainers, buckles, and retractors. If the fabric looks worn, stretched, cut, or fatigued, or if the protective plastic covers of the guides show any type of wear, replacement of the entire seat belt assembly (buckle and retractor) will be necessary.

All about air bags

The air bag system is one of the most effective auto safety systems ever invented. Most cars built since 1994 have at least a driver's-side air bag, and almost all newer cars have both driver- and passenger-side air bags as standard equipment.

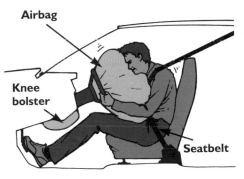

The system consists of several components, including sensors to detect the rapid deceleration caused by a frontal impact, a knee bolster on the driver's side to help absorb energy, and a collapsible steering column. The system kicks in if an impact equals or exceeds the force of a collision between a car traveling at 10 to 14 MPH and a solid wall. The sensors trigger an inflator, which causes a solid chemical propellant to undergo a rapid chemical change that produces nitrogen gas. The gas quickly inflates the woven nylon airbag, which inflates fully in about 1/20 second. It begins to deflate immediately so that you won't suffocate, and to allow you to leave the vehicle as quickly as possible.

A couple of warnings are in order, however. Air bags don't eliminate the need for wearing safety belts, and they're effective only in frontal collisions (though some cars also have side air bags). Also, you should never place a child in the front seat of a vehicle equipped with a passenger-side air bag; recent evidence shows that the force of an expanding airbag can injure or even kill small passengers.

Playing it safe

Squelch that static shock!

Zapped by static as you slide out of your car? It comes from what you're wearing: rubbing against the upholstery generates static electricity. A static charge can contain as much as 25,000 volts (most people can feel the zap at about 4,000 volts), and even a 100-volt jolt can damage a car's electronic circuitry.

To prevent the shock, ground yourself: Keep your hand on the metal door until *after* you've touched ground with your foot.

Keep your firefighter fit

A fire extinguisher in your car is a great idea, but store it right. Temperatures in a car baking in the summer sun can soar, damaging the extinguisher. Units manufactured in the last 10 years that carry the Underwriters Laboratories (UL) logo have passed overheating tests. Even so, keep any fire extinguisher in the trunk, out of direct sunlight. Don't let it roll around back there, either; most come with a mounting bracket. Buy a unit that has a pressure gauge and be sure to check it every month.

Installing a cellular phone holder

If you have a cellular phone, it probably slides from one side of the car to the other, and you might crash as you chase it. The solution is to buy a phone holster from an electronics store. Installation is simple.

Hold the base in various spots. You want the phone to be accessible but not in the way of accessories or controls. It's best to mount the baseplate to the floor, but it can go on any solid surface as long as there's at least 1 inch of clearance behind the mounting plate. Drill three holes using the base as a template, and then mount it with the supplied screws (place a dab of clear caulk on the screws to seal the holes).

Tip: Have a bag phone that won't fit into a holder? Place some Velcro on the back of the phone's carrying case to secure it to the carpet. This setup is also great for a portable CB radio or CD player.

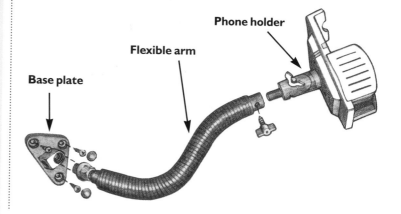

Phone holder

Flexible arm

Base plate

Do-it-yourself auto security system

Auto security systems with just a siren and sensor can be basic and cheap (less than $75), or you can add features and take the price over $500. Complex systems can disable the ignition system, yell "Please step away from the car," lock the doors automatically, and trigger a transmitter to call you for help. The high-end systems call for professional installation, but you can install a basic system, such as the one shown here, yourself. It's easy (really!) and requires only an hour using common tools.

Mount the basic unit where it can be well grounded (near or on metal), close to the front of your car so the siren will be loudest. Find a spot that's reasonably protected from both moisture and engine or radiator heat. Try to use an existing bolt or screw to hold it in place, rather than drill any holes. If necessary, run a separate wire to ground the unit.

Place a heavy rag over the siren before connecting the red wire to the positive cable or terminal of the battery. Adjust the shock/motion sensor according to the manufacturer's instructions, and arm the unit with the remote keypad to test it. Remove the rag once you're satisfied the alarm is working properly. You're done.

Some installation notes: On units that have an antenna wire, make sure it's straight and as far away from metal as possible. And if your vehicle has an electric cooling fan that runs when the ignition is off, clip the over-three-minute delay wire. If you have headlights that shut off automatically and no fan delay, clip the 3-minute delay wire. An alarm system is triggered when it senses a change in the electrical system's voltage; that could be the dome light going on . . . or a cooling fan.

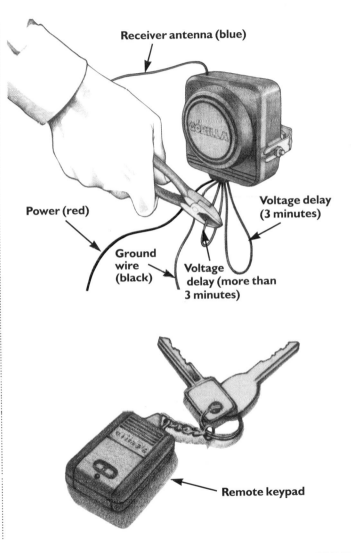

Receiver antenna (blue)

Power (red)

Ground wire (black)

Voltage delay (3 minutes)

Voltage delay (more than 3 minutes)

Remote keypad

Emergencies: Prepare and repair

If you're ever in an accident . . .

No one relishes the thought of an auto accident, but being prepared can ease the tension and confusion. Here's a list of what to have on hand and what to do. Copy this page and put it in your glove compartment; if you're a bit shaken after an accident (who wouldn't be?), the following list will help you regain composure.

Keep in the vehicle:

✔Name of insurance company and your agent's phone number (home and business).

✔ Phone number of a local towing company, dealer, or body shop you trust. This may save you from the hassle and expense of towing your car twice, or finding your vehicle being held hostage for repairs by the towing firm.

✔ Notepad and pencil

✔First-aid kit

✔Blanket

After the accident:

• Stop your car and shut it off.

• If no one is injured in your car, and if it's unsafe to remain there, get everyone out and away from the vehicle and other traffic.

• Don't move anyone who is injured unless there is a life-threatening situation at hand (fire, possible further injury, or leaking gasoline, for example). If you know first aid, use it.

• Call the police (here's where cellular phones come in handy) or have someone else call. If there are injuries, call 911 first.

• If the vehicles are drivable and pose a hazard to others, move them to the side of the road.

• Get witnesses' phone numbers (especially those of people not involved in the accident).

• Get the names, addresses, and driver's license numbers of those involved in the accident.

• Make a list of observable injuries.

• Write down the name of each driver's insurance company, agent, and the make of each car and its license plate number.

• Sketch the scene on a piece of paper, or take pictures to document the scene. Document the position of the vehicles, their direction of travel, warning or traffic signs, time of day, and road and weather conditions.

• Later, complete a police accident report if there were injuries, or any other state or provincial reports if there were no injuries.

After everything else is done:

• Notify your insurance agent.

• If the vehicle is undrivable, call a towing service, but do not authorize repairs.

• Finally, *don't* accuse, argue, or admit guilt; *don't* sign anything without reading it well; and *don't* finalize your insurance claim until all bills are in and the repairs are completed to your satisfaction.

What to do if the engine overheats

That billowing cloud of steam from the front of the car, and the ominous flashing light on the dashboard or needle stuck in the red zone of your engine's temperature gauge, both mean the same thing: The engine is on the verge of meltdown.

Cool down the engine before it goes nuclear and it'll probably escape permanent harm. Here's what to do:

1 Turn off the air conditioner and turn on the heater full-blast. This pulls heat from the engine. If you're in stop-and-go traffic, take the next exit or side road so you can drive faster to get air moving through the **radiator**. Even if the engine begins to cool back to normal, stop soon to check the coolant level.

2 If the engine continues to get hotter or if steam is coming from the engine compartment, pull off the road, shut off the engine, and open the hood. Wait 20 minutes before inspecting the radiator and hoses for leaks—they are really hot! Refill the radiator after another 20-minute wait. Add water or coolant by pouring it into the overflow tank. (Never add either to a *hot* engine unless the engine is running; you could damage the engine block.) If there's no overflow tank, flip up the lever of the radiator cap with a heavy rag or loosen it slightly; then quickly stand back. If the radiator is still steaming, let it cool before adding water or coolant.

3 With the hood still up, start the engine and examine the radiator and hoses for leaks. You can sometimes jury-rig a fix for a leaky hose (see p. 15) that will get you to a service station. If you can't fix the hose, or if the radiator is leaking (or if the engine won't start), call a tow truck. If you continue to run an engine that's overheating, you'll destroy it.

(see p. 15)

Quick tip
Key hideout behind the license plate

If you've ever locked your keys in the car or lost them, you know exasperation firsthand. Memory tonics aren't yet available, but here's something that will make the predicament less of a problem.

Have an extra key made for the car door, and hide it behind the license plate. Simply remove one of the screws that hold the plate in place, put the key behind the plate, and retighten the screw with a coin. It's there when you need it, yet it's also hidden.

Attach through hole in key

License plate bolt

PNN 140

Emergencies: Prepare and repair

First aid for a dragging exhaust system

Stop immediately if you hear the awful grinding sound that means the exhaust system is dragging. It's dangerous to keep driving: The offending pipe or **muffler** can wedge itself under your vehicle, or it can break free and end up in the path of another car. Here's what to do next.

Make sure both wheels are well up on curb

1. Drive carefully up onto a curb so that one side of the vehicle is raised. Make sure the vehicle is completely and safely on the curb. Never try to work under any car or truck that's supported by a tire jack.

That awful grinding sound? It's your car telling you to pull over right away.

2. Take a look at the situation. A dragging muffler or broken tailpipe is usually due to a broken hanger. If that's the case, find a way to tie up and support the exhaust system, at least long enough to get it properly repaired, to avoid further damage.

Hot!

Gloves

Broken hangers

Rag

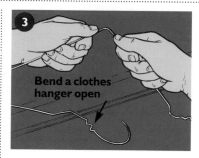

Bend a clothes hanger open

3. Finding something to support a dragging pipe is usually easy. Rope, elastic cords, or even a straightened coat hanger will work. If you don't have something in your vehicle, check the roadside trash or a nearby business or home.

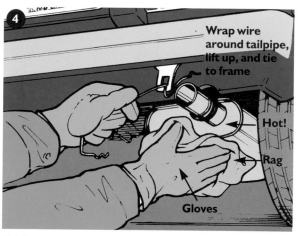

Wrap wire around tailpipe, lift up, and tie to frame

Hot!

Rag

Gloves

4. Wrap the wire or cord around the tailpipe; then feed the wire through any nearby bracket while as you lift the muffler. Don't wrap anything around the **driveshaft**! Wear gloves or use a thick layer of rags to protect your hands. Remember: this is only a temporary fix. Get the exhaust system properly repaired immediately.

Emergency hose repairs

The first hint of trouble is the wisp of steam rising from under the hood. Clue two is the pungent aroma of **antifreeze**. Before you know it, you're stranded. What now?

Well, if you have an emergency kit in the trunk, you'll be back on the road again soon. Stash these tools and products in a box or a plastic bucket:

✔ a pair of work gloves
✔ a jackknife or utility knife
✔ slotted- and Phillips-head screwdrivers
✔ a few hose clamps
✔ a large pair of pliers
✔ two types of hose repair kits (**radiator** hoses are about 2 inches in diameter; heater hoses are less than an inch in diameter)
✔ the old hoses from the last time you had the hoses changed
✔ a gallon jug containing a 50:50 mix of water and antifreeze
✔ a flashlight, with extra batteries still in their package

Quick hose repairs. Before attacking the problem, let the engine cool down. Make sure you and the vehicle are in a safe position. Wearing gloves, slowly and carefully open the radiator cap to release the pressure.

If the leak is near the end of a hose, just on the other side of a clamp, your best bet is to shorten the hose. Loosen the clamp and slide it out of the way. Slice the hose from its edge to the damage (see inset, right) and peel it off the outlet. Slip the hose back onto the fitting, slide the clamp in place, and tighten it. Top off the coolant system from your jug.

Bigger problems. Unfortunately, many hose failures don't occur near the clamp. That's when you need an inexpensive hose repair kit. The kits for heater or radiator hoses cost less than $20 each at an auto parts store, and include a pair of hose clamps with two different size couplings. Just cut out the damaged section of hose, slip the exposed ends of the remaining hose onto a coupling, and install the hose clamps. Add coolant and you'll be on your way.

Complete hose failure. If a hose ruptures, making any type of repair impossible, those old spare hoses will be priceless. Let the engine cool, remove the clamps, and pull off the damaged hose. Slip the spare into place, tighten the clamps, and add coolant.

Heater hoses. Your engine really doesn't need to circulate **coolant** through the heater core for safe operation, so immediate repair is not absolutely necessary. Instead, you can cut the damaged section of hose and plug the open ends with bolts, tool handles, even spare spark plugs; anything solid, clamped securely in place, will get you back on the road.

While any of these repairs will get you moving again, they're temporary only. Head directly to a service station for a permanent repair job and full replacement of lost coolant.

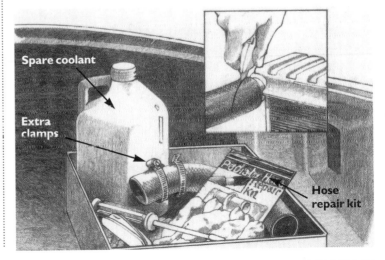

Spare coolant

Extra clamps

Hose repair kit

Surviving winter

Don't let the cold catch *you*

If you live where the winters are mild, count your blessings: Cold, snowy winters are tough on cars. Wintertime travel can be risky, too, if severe cold or heavy snow leaves you stranded. That's why it's a good idea to reduce the chances of having problems in the first place. How? Follow this checklist:

Under the hood

✔ Change the oil and filter before winter's onset. Use the grade and weight recommended in your owner's manual (see p.32).

✔ Check the coolant for a 50:50 antifreeze and water mix, which protects down to well below 0°F. If the coolant is more than 2 years/24,000 miles old, you should drain it, flush the system, and install fresh coolant.

✔ Check hoses and drive belts for cracks, fraying, or obvious signs of age. Replace any that are more than 4 years old. Check the tension of belts (see p.88).

✔ Clean and check the battery cable connections and the battery water level. Many batteries come with 72- to 80-month guarantees, but replacing one earlier is relatively cheap insurance against getting stranded.

✔ Check all fluid levels (oil, transmission, brakes, windshield washer). Add windshield washer antifreeze/cleaner. Automatic transmission fluid should be changed every 2 years or 24,000 miles.

✔ Newer cars need an annual emission tune-up (see p.78). At the same time, have the spark plugs inspected and replaced if needed. Have the engine performance electronically "scoped".

Around the car

✔ Check tires, including the spare, for cuts, cracks, or other damage. Inflate them to the right pressure. Replace worn tires.

✔ Check all the lights and turn signals. Replace any bulbs.

✔ Replace the wiper blades.

✔ Have your brake system inspected as part of your pre-winter preparations.

✔ Lubricate all door locks with spray lubricant to prevent freeze-ups.

Inside the car

✔ Clean all glass to reduce fogging (see p.154).

✔ Lightly lubricate door/trunk rubber gaskets with a silicone paste (keep it away from paint).

✔ Test the heater and defroster to make sure they're working properly. Warm up the car; then operate all the heat and defrost controls and feel for the heat.

Winter survival kit

You're going to need more than a windshield scraper to get past winter's worst; here's a basic survival kit. You may also want to pack a fire extinguisher and a sleeping bag.

- ✓ Jumper cables (see p.119)
- ✓ Flashlight and spare batteries
- ✓ Emergency flares
- ✓ Spare gloves, boots, overalls or jacket, blanket, hat
- ✓ Traction aids such as sand, gravel, cat litter, or tire chains. Four three-tab asphalt roofing shingles placed rough side up under the stuck drive wheel(s) provide almost 6 feet of traction, yet take up almost no room in the trunk because they lie flat
- ✓ Moisture-displacing spray lubricant WD-40 ✓
- ✓ Aerosol can of tire sealer/inflator (get a brand that doesn't use a flammable propellant)

- ✓ Quarters for a pay phone
- ✓ Windshield scraper and brush
- ✓ Small shovel
- ✓ Tools: slotted and Phillips screwdrivers; hammer; adjustable wrench; pliers; Torx drivers (#15 and #20); jacknife.
- ✓ Duct tape, spare fuses
- ✓ Candle stubs (or canned heat) and matches for light, a little warmth, and heating liquids
- ✓ Large plastic garbage bags (great weather protection)
- ✓ An orange or bright red bandanna or cloth to put on your antenna as a distress signal
- ✓ Some nonperishable snacks and a small can opener

Hope for the best but prepare for the worst.

Keeping your engine warm

If winter temperatures regularly skid below 15° F in your area, consider installing an engine heater. It'll save wear and tear on engine parts, help the engine to start easily, and let the interior warm up faster too! There's a variety of plug-in heaters available. Here's the lowdown:

Freeze plug heater. A heating element mounted in the engine block's cooling jacket. Inexpensive (less than $20) and efficient, but in most cases it requires dealer installation, which isn't cheap.

Lower radiator hose heater. A thermostat controls a heating element located in the lower radiator hose where it directly heats the engine coolant. It offers high efficiency and is easy to install.

Magnetic heater. Mounted on a steel oil pan, a magnetic heater heats the oil. Thermostatically controlled and reasonably efficient. It costs less than $30 and can be used on more than one vehicle, but only those with steel oil pans .

Dipstick heater. Just install it in place of the original dipstick. It's usable on more than one vehicle and inexpensive ($10 to $15). It's not as efficient as the others, but it's better than nothing.

Battery heater. A warm battery has more power for cold-engine starts. These electric blankets (less than $30) fit under or around the battery and keep it toasty. They work well if the battery is in decent shape.

Surviving winter

Freeing a frozen lock

A frozen car lock can be terribly frustrating. Though you may be tempted, don't try to force the lock open or you might break the key off in the cylinder (then you'll *really* be in a pickle). Instead, try the other door—you'd be amazed at how many people don't think of this simple solution. If that doesn't work, try one (or more) of the following lock-freeing tricks.

Thaw a frozen lock by heating the key with a cigarette lighter or matches. Wear gloves or use pliers to hold the key. As soon as it's warm, immediately put it in the lock and try it. You may have to repeat this several times until you get results.

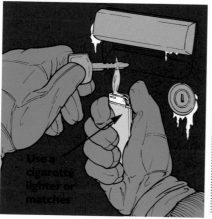

Use a cigarette lighter or matches

Electric hair dryer

Spray lock deicer into the key opening. The small packages of deicer are effective and inexpensive but won't do you much good if you store them in the glove compartment inside the locked car.

Thawing will be even faster if you're home and close to an outlet. Just plug in a hand-held hair dryer and aim it at the frozen lock.

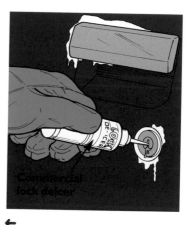

Commercial lock deicer

Prevent lock freeze-ups with lubricant. Periodic applications of a moisture-displacing spray lubricant will ensure smooth operation. If your vehicle spends a lot of time going through car washes during cold weather, take a few seconds to spray some into the lock immediately after each wash.

WD 40

Getting unstuck

Getting stuck now and then in snow, mud, ice, or sand is, unfortunately, a fact of life. Read on and you'll discover that there's a right way and a wrong away to get unstuck.

Try some patience first. Once you realize you're stuck, stop immediately and analyze the situation. If you packed traction aids (see p. 17), put them to work.

Take your time. Even if you don't have any traction helpers in the trunk, it may be possible to drive out if the drive wheels aren't buried to the hubs. Turn off the radio and open a window on each side so you can listen for wheel spin. With the engine idling, gently apply just a touch of power.

If you remembered to pack emergency traction aids, pat yourself on the back!

If it moves. Don't add more power and spin the tires. Let the car continue as far as possible. The trick is careful use of the throttle to avoid wheel spin. Once the wheels are out of the holes, nurse the car back onto solid ground.

If it doesn't. If the tires spin, try "rocking" the car with the throttle. Slowly push the throttle to the point of wheel spin— a car often moves fractionally just before the tires lose traction—then let up on the gas the instant they spin. As the car rolls back into the holes, gently squeeze the gas again to get a rocking effect. The trick is to press on the gas to coincide with the change in direction.

With good timing and a bit of luck, the vehicle may rock back and forth just enough to regain traction. Getting the car to rock is easy if it has a manual transmission, because you can control it with the clutch. With automatics, you'll probably need to shift between *Forward* and *Reverse*. What you also must do, however, is use the brakes to keep the car from slipping backwards and let the engine settle back to idle before shifting gears.

Be gentle with your car. Slamming the shifter from *Forward* to *Reverse* is incredibly hard on any **transmission** and generates enormous heat. Spinning the wheels also generates lots of heat, sometimes enough to kill the tires. And if one tire is spinning and the other isn't, tires *and* the **differential** are taking a beating (see p. 94).

Recognize defeat. If you just can't free the car, call a tow truck. Professional towing is hundreds of dollars cheaper than buying new tires or repairing a **transmission, clutch,** or **differential.**

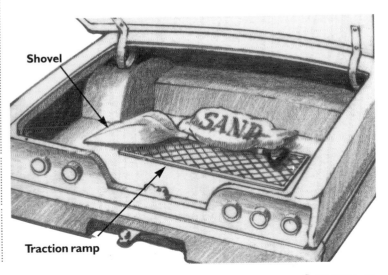

Shovel

Traction ramp

Troubleshooting in a nutshell

Identifying leaks

Many different fluids leak out of your car. To help identify them, place a plastic container where the leak occurs, or if the leak is very small, a piece of white paper to capture its color.

Leaks are identified by physical evidence—smell, color, texture, etc. Once the source is identified, sometimes simply tightening a clamp or bolt may solve the problem.

Antifreeze: Usually green or yellow (the new Dex-Cool stuff is bright orange) liquid with a sweet pungent odor. Old **coolant** will be rusty or dirty brown. Look for leaks at the radiator, upper and lower **radiator** hoses, heater hoses, and engine core plugs.

Automatic-transmission fluid: Usually a light red or brownish red oil. Compare it to the color, smell, and feel of the oil on the **transmission** dipstick. Check around the pan and external seals for leakage.

Battery acid: If it has a rotten-egg, sulfurlike odor, it's probably sulfuric acid leaking from the battery. Highly corrosive—if it touches skin or clothing, flush immediately with water.

Brake fluid: Clear, thin, almost waterlike. Leaking brake fluid is a danger sign requiring immediate attention. Get to a mechanic!

Diesel fuel: The aroma is almost the same as home heating oil. Check the injector pump, fuel filter, and fuel lines.

Gasoline: Obvious by its unmistakable sharp, acrid odor. Extremely poisonous. Check under the hood, at the fuel tank, and along all fuel lines.

Gear oil: A heavyweight oil, usually dark or black (a light tan when fresh). Used in manual transmissions, axles, and **differentials**; may show up on the CV axle boots of front-wheel-drive vehicles.

Grease: Very thick, sticky. Minor leakage after a routine grease job is normal.

Power-steering fluid: Older cars used automatic-transmission fluid in the steering system. Newer cars use special power-steering fluid that's almost the same color as fresh motor oil, but is slightly thinner and has a distinctly different smell. Fluid that turns silvery gray indicates an internal failure of the power-steering system. Have this checked out as soon as possible.

Shock absorber fluid: It usually shows up as a dark stain on the shock body itself. Check all shocks. If leakage is found, replace the shock.

Water: If it looks and smells like clear water, it's condensation from the air conditioner.

Windshield washer solvent: Bluish in color, it smells of detergent or alcohol. Persistent leakage indicates a cracked fluid reservoir or a leaking hose between the reservoir and the windshield washer nozzles. Washer solvent is poisonous.

Oil   Water   Coolant   Transmission fluid

Not so funny noises

Your ears often provide the first warning of car trouble. Here's how to recognize the meaning of what you hear ...

From the engine
Noise: Squealing
Source: Loose or worn drive belt.

Noise: Continuous hum or whine that may get louder at times.
Source: The **alternator** or **water pump**, or if the whine gets louder as you turn the steering wheel, the power-steering pump.

Noise: Deep rhythmical thumping or thudding.
Source: A bad-news noise. The engine's main or rod bearings are the likely suspects.

Noise: Soft, rhythmical slapping that may stop as the engine warms up.
Source: Called "piston slap," it's OK as long as it goes away once the engine is warm.

Noise: Irregular snapping or clicking, along with a rough-running engine or a loss of power.
Source: Electrical arcing in the distributor cap or spark plugs.

Noise: Pinging.
Source: Engine out of tune; may need higher-**octane** gas.

From the suspension
Noise: Clunks, pops, and rattles in response to road bumps.
Source: Could be suspension and steering components, or loose exhaust system parts.

Noise: Grinding or growling sound noticeable when turning.
Source: The wheel bearings are the most likely cause.

Noise: Rhythmical metallic click while driving.
Source: Loose hubcap or wheel bearing.

From the exhaust
Noise: Sudden increase in exhaust noise volume or tone.

Source: Failed **muffler** or a hole somewhere in the exhaust system. The louder the sound, the farther forward the damage.

From the brakes
Noise: Light squeaking on light to medium brake applications.
Source: Relatively normal characteristic of disc brakes. If heard when brakes *aren't* in use, the brake wear indicators are announcing "Time for servicing!"

Noise: Occasional heavy grinding or groaning.
Source: Can be normal, or can be brake dust trapped in the pads.

Noise: High-pitched squeaking whenever brakes are applied.
Source: Loose brake pad, or glazed pads or rotor/drum.

Noise: Chattering as brakes are applied.
Source: Contaminated or broken **brake pads**, or **brake rotors** and drums that are out of round.

From the transmission or drivetrain
Noise: Whine or howl, most evident in *Park* or *Neutral*.
Source: A damaged hydraulic pump in the **transmission** or the **torque converter**.

Noise: Progressively louder clicking as the steering wheel in a front-wheel-drive vehicle is turned.
Source: Faulty **constant velocity** (CV) **joint**.

Noise: Resonant howl or whine only when accelerating or decelerating.
Source: Dry or damaged differential gears and bearings.

n theory, you can fix just about anything with only the most basic of tools. Of course reality has a nasty way of trampling over even the tidiest of theories. If you truly want to take control of automotive maintenance tasks and some basic repairs, you'll need more than a roll of duct tape. Nothing exotic, mind you—just a reasonable selection of tools and common mechanical gizmos to help get the easily done stuff done right. After all, why should you waste your time trying to figure out how to make that rusty pair of pliers double as a torque wrench? In the following pages you'll find out how to choose and use just the tools you'll need in order to work safely and efficiently.

Tools for safety

Working safely under your car

Working underneath a vehicle is never a lot of fun, and it can also be dangerous. Here's how to do it safely:

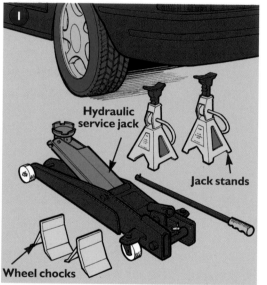

Hydraulic service jack

Jack stands

Wheel chocks

1. You'll won't spend a lot for everything you need. Get at least two ratcheting jack stands, a set of **wheel chocks** (you can make your own), and a hydraulic service jack. The jack stands and service jack should be rated to exceed the weight of your vehicle. You can use drive-up ramps instead (not shown), but only if you won't be working on the wheels, brakes, or suspension. *Never* work under any vehicle supported only by the car's factory-supplied jack—it's only for tire changes! Once you're ready to set up, find a level area to work on.

2. Position the service jack so that its saddle (the part that contacts the vehicle) will not damage any components. Your owner's manual may show the specific jacking points. Wheels not being raised should have chocks placed against them. Pump the jack up slowly as you move it into position.

Release valve

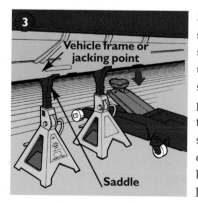

Vehicle frame or jacking point

Saddle

3. Ratchet each jack stand saddle up into place, and then slowly lower the service jack until the jack stands are solidly supporting the vehicle. Never put additional saddles on either the service jack or the jack stands because they can slip off—and you wouldn't want to be underneath a car when that happens!

Wrenches

The A-B-Sees of car work

Always wear eye protection when working on your car—it's your best defense against flying debris and chemical splashes. Put safety eyewear in your toolbox; if it's handy, you'll wear it. *Don't* rely on ordinary prescription eyeglasses: True safety lenses are stamped with the manufacturer's logo to indicate they have passed impact tests. Polycarbonate lenses are the most impact-resistant.

✔ If you buy only one pair of eye protection, get goggles. They're inexpensive and provide full eye protection; many can be worn over prescription glasses. "Direct vent" models allow good air circulation and minimize fogging; "indirect vent" models provide more protection against fine particles or splashes.

✔ Non-prescription safety glasses cost as little as $5.

The side shields on some models block particles from entering at the sides, but safety glasses don't protect as well as goggles.

Prescription safety glasses ($75 to $300) are ideal for those who always wear glasses anyway. Polycarbonate models with side shields offer the best protection. Their frames are more rugged than ordinary eyeglass frames.

Direct-vent goggles

Elastic strap

Safety glasses

Side shields

Socket wrenches

The Do-It-Yourself Creed states: "The number of skinned knuckles on your hand is inversely proportional to the size of your socket set." A socket wrench set (a driver and numerous sockets) is the most important repair tool you'll use. A high-quality set, properly used and cared for, will last a lifetime.

The socket is the cylindrical part of the wrench that fits around a nut or bolt. The inside has either 6 points (best for gripping bolts with rounded corners) or 12 points (easiest to use in tight quarters). Sockets are available in standard (SAE) sizes (in $\frac{1}{16}$- and $\frac{1}{32}$-inch increments) and in metric sizes (in 1-millimeter increments). You'll need both because most foreign and domestically built vehicles contain metric fasteners. Deep sockets are ideal for removing spark plugs, nuts with bolts protruding through them, and recessed fasteners.

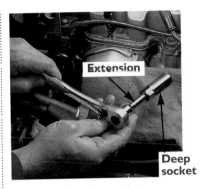

Extension

Deep socket

The driver is what turns the socket. A socket driver must be turned like a screwdriver. A ratchet driver is faster—you can swing it back and forth to tighten or remove fasteners. Extensions are bars that extend your reach.

Drive size refers to the square recess in the back of the socket and the mating surface on a driver. The most common sizes are $\frac{1}{4}$ inch, $\frac{3}{8}$ inch, and $\frac{1}{2}$ inch. Start your tool collection with a $\frac{3}{8}$-inch drive set and add others as needed. A set that can turn bolts from $\frac{3}{8}$ to $\frac{7}{8}$ inch and 6 to 19 millimeters will handle most jobs.

Wrenches

Success with socket wrenches

Having the right tool is one thing; using it right is quite another. Here are tips for using this all-important tool properly:

✔ Pick sockets that fit the nut or bolt exactly. If you use one that's just ¹⁄₁₆ inch or 1 millimeter too large, you risk rounding the head of the bolt or nut.

✔ To install spark plugs, use a special spark plug socket; it has a rubber retainer inside to grip the plug and keep it centered.

✔ Keep an eye on where your hands might hit if the wrench or bolt suddenly lets go.

✔ Cheater bars—lengths of pipe slipped over wrench handles to increase leverage—can often loosen stubborn bolts. But beware; they can also overpower the ratchet mechanism and destroy a socket or wrench.

✔ OK, OK, by this point in your life you probably know which way to turn nuts and bolts, but if not, recite this little ditty: "Right to tight, left to loose."

Accessories, gizmos, and care
You can tighten or remove almost

Ratchet driver

Phillips bit

any nut or bolt, regardless of how stubborn or awkwardly located, with the proper accessory. Here are the most useful gizmos:

✔ Adapters allow sockets of one drive size (say, ¼ inch) to fit onto a ratchet wrench of a larger drive size (say, ⅜ inch).

✔ Extensions fit between the wrench and the socket for reaching recessed or buried fasteners.

✔ Spinner discs, small ribbed discs placed between the wrench and the socket, can be spun by hand. Use them to quickly tighten or loosen fasteners when leverage isn't needed.

✔ A flex-head ratchet provides access to confined or awkwardly located fasteners.

✔ Bit sockets for driving **Torx**- and Phillips-head screws are increasingly popular. A Phillips bit grasped by a small socket (see photo at left) allows you to reach screws in tricky places.

✔ Store sockets and drivers away from moisture, and wipe them clean after each use. Give the working mechanism of ratchet drivers an occasional shot of WD-40 or a similar cleaning and lubricating product.

Quick tip
Order in the case

There's a simple way to keep all your sockets in order and in their case. Cut a piece of ½-inch-thick foam rubber to fit inside the lid and glue it into place. When you fasten the catch, all the sockets will stay securely where they belong.

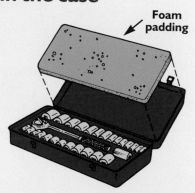

Foam padding

Choosing the right wrench

Wrenches come in many shapes, sizes, and configurations. Described here are four basic types: open-end, box-end, combination, and adjustable. Each type of wrench (see drawings, right) has its own advantages and disadvantages.

Open-end wrenches. These have open jaws at both ends, each with a different size opening. The openings allow the wrench to slip over nuts or bolts in tight spaces. The angled head allows the wrench to be flipped over after each turn to maintain good contact between the jaws and the bolt head. Open-end wrenches should not be used for final tightening or removing tight bolts, however. The weak jaws can spread open, round off a bolt head, or slip off.

Box-end wrenches. These babies are longer and stronger than either open-end or combination wrenches. Both ends, each a different size, fit completely around a nut or bolt. Because they grip all six sides of a bolt head, they're used for final tightening and for removing extremely tight or rusted nuts and bolts. They come in both 6- and 12-point designs.

Combination wrenches. Ahh, the best of both worlds. These wrenches have one open end and one box end of the same size. They're slightly longer than an open-end wrench.

Adjustable wrench. The jaws of an adjustable wrench move in and out to fit different size nuts and bolts. When it comes to working on cars, though, use an adjustable wrench only when no other wrench will fit, because its jaws are relatively weak. It can also serve as the one wrench you keep in the car for emergencies.

Nuts about wrenches

No matter what kind of wrench you have or how many of them, sooner or later you'll meet some nut that just doesn't want to cooperate. Maybe it's playing hide-and-seek way down in the bowels of the engine compartment, or maybe it's just rusted solid. Well, here are a few tricks for putting those #*&!! nuts in their place.

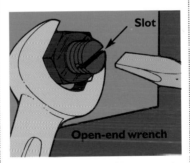

Can't reach the bolt? You can often tighten a bolt even though it's impossible to reach the bolt head. It's easy if you hacksaw a slot in the bottom end of the bolt. Then insert your screwdriver in the saw slot to hold the bolt while you turn the nut.

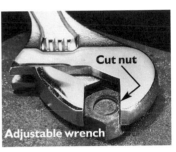

Nut rusty? Use a hacksaw to cut one side of the nut. Split the nut with a cold chisel and remove it with an adjustable wrench.

Space tight? If there's no room to start a nut, stick tape on the back of a wrench and place the nut in the wrench. The tape will hold the nut long enough for you to get things started.

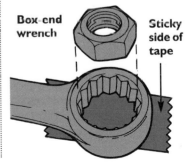

Screwdrivers

Screwdriver tips (and techniques)

Screwdrivers are one tool just about everyone has. Still, not everyone has the right one; here's what to look for.

The most familiar types are the straight blade and the Phillips blade. A screwdriver with a straight blade fits a screwhead that has a slot. The Phillips has a four-prong tip that fits into a star or cross-shaped screw slot. The four contact surfaces make removal and installation of a Phillips screw easier than a slotted screw because the screwdriver is less likely to slip. The working end, or tip, of a Phillips screwdriver determines its size: No. 1 is the smallest; No. 2 (the most familiar size) is a bit larger.

Pozidriv and **Torx** are two specialty screwdrivers now in widespread use. Pozidriv screwdrivers are very similar to the Phillips but have a blunter tip and eight contact points for a better grip. The six-prong tip of a Torx driver provides more turning force with less slippage. Torx-head screws secure most outside trim on a vehicle (including headlamps, mirrors, and luggage racks), while Pozidriv screws secure most of the trim inside. Torx

Bad drivers are a menace (and not just on streets and golf courses).

screwdrivers come in many different sizes, but numbers 15 and 20 are the most commonly used these days.

Screwdrivers come in a dizzying array of lengths and configurations. One-inch stubby models and offset screwdrivers are great for getting into tight places; monster screwdrivers 3 feet long reach screws in difficult spots. The best screwdrivers have large-diameter handles and shanks for more turning power.

The handles should also be insulated (plastic or covered with rubber) so they won't conduct electricity. Rough-textured blade tips provide a strong grip in the screwhead; magnetized tips are great for holding small screws.

A screwdriver's blade should completely fill the slot on the screwhead. Using the wrong size blade may damage the screw or cause the tool to slip. Never use a screwdriver as a pry bar, chisel, or punch. Screwdriver handles are too weak to withstand the constant pounding of a hammer, and the blade shanks aren't strong enough for prying.

Don't use a screwdriver if the tip is chipped, the handle is damaged, or the shank is loose.

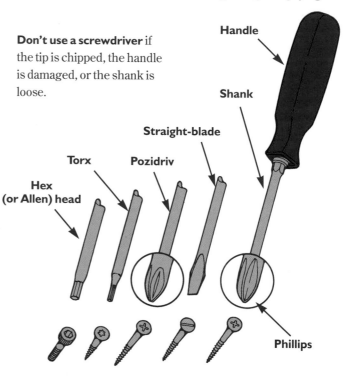

Handle

Shank

Straight-blade

Torx   Pozidriv

Hex
(or Allen) head

Phillips

Screw gripper

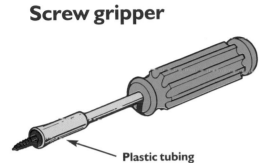

Plastic tubing

Here's how to install screws in tight places: slide a length of plastic tubing about 3 inches long over the blade of your screwdriver so one end of the tubing just grips the screwhead. Now you can position the screw without having to hold it. For ordinary screwdriving, slide the tubing up the shaft so it's out of the way.

A handy unscrewer for tight spaces

An engine compartment is a cluttered place, and sometimes there's just no way to reach a screw using a standard, straight-shank screwdriver. That's when you need an offset screwdriver. This little Z-shaped gem has a Phillips (or slotted) tip at each end, and you can reach it into just about anywhere.

Palm saver for screwdriver

Save your palms from blisters when bearing down on a screwdriver. Hold the plastic top from a spray paint can over the screwdriver's handle. The cap, not your palm, will take the twisting pressure, and it will also help you hold the screwdriver straight.

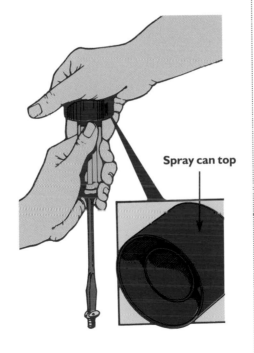

Spray can top

Quick tip

True grip

To get a better grip on your plastic-handle screwdrivers, slip a rubber chair leg tip over the handle. The tip will improve your leverage and cushion your hand. You can get one at just about any hardware store.

At the other end of a screwdriver is another type of problem. The screwdriver's blade will usually slip out of a worn screwhead, particularly if it's a slotted screw but even if it's a Phillips. That's not only frustrating but costly (it grinds down the screwdriver's tip) and dangerous. First, try to clean out any debris that might be plugging up the screw slots. Then, to reduce slippage, dab a bit of valve grinding compound (available at your auto parts supplier), on the blade of your screwdriver to get a really good grip. Be sure to push down firmly on the screwdriver as you turn it; you'll probably be rewarded for your patience and ingenuity with a fastener that finally begins to back out.

Chapter 3

Fluids, Lubes, and Filters

Oil truly is "black gold." It's so valuable to engines, in fact, that without the stuff we'd still be riding horses down to the mall (although presumably parking would be easier to find).

Like many things automotive, there's a lot of misinformation and mythology associated with oil. Can you use recycled oil? Yep. Will synthetic oils really last for 25,000 miles? Sure, but don't wait that long before changing it. What's good about dirty oil? Dirt shows that the oil is working the way it should, but too dirty isn't good.

Your car or truck needs more lubricants and fluids than just oil, too, and you'd better know what (and where) they are if you want to enjoy trouble free motoring. There's a chart in this chapter that will show you exactly which lubrication jobs you've probably forgotten, and plenty of other slick information as well.

Oil and oil filters

Here's oil you need to know

Is it Greek, or do all those letters on a can of motor oil actually mean something in English? Here's a translation guide:

✔ API signifies the American Petroleum Institute's (API) service rating for motor oil.

✔ SF, SG, SH, and SJ (the newest) are performance standards set by the API. Each letter designation increase signifies a newer, higher standard of oil, with more additives. You can always use a higher-designated oil (SH instead of SF), but *never* use an oil with a lower rating.

✔ Oil classifications that start with the letter C indicate motor oils for diesel engines.

✔ SAE stands for Society of Automotive Engineers, the organization that designates the viscosity grading system for oil.

✔ W represents winter, meaning the oil meets **viscosity** requirements for cold weather.

✔ Number 10, 20, or 30 indicates the viscosity, or weight, of oil. Low-numbered oil is thinner than higher-numbered ("heavier") oil.

✔ "Energy conserving II" classifies oil that improves fuel economy an average of 2.7%.

Motor oil, an engine's lifeblood, is truly an amazing substance and is being improved all the time. It cleans, lubricates, cools, and cushions moving engine parts while holding sludge and chemical contaminants in suspension until your next oil change. Plus, oil has the ability to increase fuel economy and to prevent the buildup of deposits, rust, corrosion, and oxidation. Motor oil is made up of about 80% to 90% base stock (lubricant), with the rest being active ingredient additives.

Only two viscosities are recommended for newer vehicles: SAE 5W-30 and SAE 10W-30. These multigrade oils can perform in a wide range of temperatures. Multigrade 5W-30

flows easier at lower ambient (outside) temperatures. Oil rated 10W-30 is necessary when ambient temperatures are likely to be 100° F or higher. Single-grade oils have temperature limitations and will not flow easily at lower temperatures, causing premature engine wear. Generally, though, it's not necessary to switch weights as the weather changes if you're using 5W-30 or 10W-30.

Most manufacturers recommend 5W-30 for their vehicles that have an overhead camshaft. Because of its fluidity, 5W-30 easily reaches the upper part of the engine, providing adequate lubrication to the camshaft. Most manufacturers recommend the use of 10W-40 in their turbo-charged engines because turbos create tremendous heat that can thin out and break down oil sooner than a regular engine. Single 30-weight oil can be used where the temperature is always above 40° F. As always, consult your vehicle owner's manual, or call your dealer, for the correct grade of oil to use.

Using recycled oil

The American Petroleum Institute (API), a trade association of oil companies, licenses the use of its logo to companies that make products conforming to its oil standards. A licensed brand of oil, whether new or recycled (re-refined), should be safe to use.

The biggest concern about recycled oil is that the old oil it started out as may have been contaminated (by diesel fuel, transmission fluid, gear oil, gasoline, or antifreeze) during the collection process. If the separating techniques used in re-refining the oil aren't correct, you end up with a faulty product. Luckily, there are a number of recycled oils that meet API standards.

Environmentally conscious DIYers have long been recycling used engine oil at their local auto service facility. Although it may seem tempting, *never* discard waste oil into your home's heating oil tank. As motor oil lubricates, it gathers and holds carbon and metallic particles in suspension. These sediments will clog up an oil burner's feed line, nozzle, and filter.

⚡ Quick tip
A good pour tip

Every time you add oil or coolant or windshield washer fluid to your car you always spill a little, right? So keep a supply of unwaxed paper cups in the garage to use as funnels. Just punch a pencil hole in the bottom of the cup.

Unwaxed paper cup with hole in bottom

One quart of waste oil can contaminate up to 2 million gallons of water. Never dispose of used oil by pouring it down a drain!

Oil and oil filters

Synthetic motor oil versus au naturel

Is synthetic motor oil really that good? And is it true that using the stuff could void your warranty? Here are the facts.

Synthetic oil has been around for over 40 years and is formulated out of hydrocarbons manufactured from natural gas or crude petroleum. It has been widely used by the U.S. military for many years, which has found it exceptional in extreme temperature conditions. Synthetic oil doesn't thicken under extreme cold, and it also stands up better than "natural" oil under extreme heat. However, the kind of cold and heat I'm talking about doesn't occur in most parts of North America. "Extreme" means a *consistent* temperature of −20° F or lower, or 100° F and higher.

What's more important for you is that synthetic oils let you go longer between oil changes. One brand, for example, is supposed to maintain its lubricating qualities for 25,000 miles, much longer than conventional oil. However, regular oil filter replacement will be necessary to remove trapped contaminants and fresh oil added (usually a quart) to bring the oil level back to the *Full* mark.

The problem is that most manufacturers say that to keep your warranty in force you must change the oil every 6 months or 6,000 miles, whichever occurs first, if you drive under ideal conditions . If you drive in severe conditions, the requirement is to change every 3 months or 3,000 miles. If you don't follow this recommendation and something happens to the engine, even if it has nothing to do with the oil, your warranty may be declared void. Having to drain synthetic oil from your

engine as often as the manufacturer requires is expensive because synthetics can be double the price of natural oil.

Natural oil blended with synthetic has become popular. It offers nearly the performance (but not the mileage) of synthetic oil at a far lower cost than pure synthetic. But maybe the best solution is to wait until the warranty expires, and *then* switch to a synthetic oil.

 **In the know**

A(dditives)-OK?

If you feel it's necessary to use an oil additive, check with your dealer to be sure it won't void your warranty. Some additives, especially some engine oil supplements, become so thick in cold temperatures that they can't flow fast enough to protect the entire engine.

Before using any additive, please read and follow all label instructions. Don't use the old "if one is good, two is better" route here. Just remember that additives aren't overhauls in a can. They are, at best, only a temporary fix.

Dirt and sludge

Excessive sludge in the engine makes it difficult for the oil pump to maintain adequate oil pressure, which can lead to costly repairs. Mechanics may allege that sludge buildup is a result in large part of paraffin-based oils, and that it's the paraffin that causes sludge. Nonsense. Sludge forms when you don't change the oil and oil filter, PCV valve, and air filter on time, or if you use a poor-quality oil.

All high-quality motor oils are made from crude oils that contain one of three hydrocarbons, one of which is paraffinic. Paraffin is not the cause of sludge, nor does it mean wax. Paraffin is the name of a family of hydrocarbons that are relatively stable and resistant to the chemical changes that take place inside an engine. This means less sludge, varnish, and corrosive wear.

Motor oil will turn black after 3,000 miles, even if there is no sludge in the engine. Dirty oil is simply proof that it's doing its job of keeping the by-products of combustion, such as carbon, in suspension so they can be drained from the engine.

The best advice about oil? Be religious about changing it according the schedule in your owner's manual.

But what can be done if a buildup of sludge occurs? Engine-cleaning additives added to the oil may eliminate sludge. Should you try some? Sure, why not? What have you got to lose? If you don't do something about the sludge, eventually you'll have some expensive engine problems. Having a mechanic remove a bunch of parts, scoop sludge from

the engine, and clean things up is not cheap. Just make sure you use national brand–name additives. An alternative is to step up your oil/filter change interval and be sure the oil is warm (not hot) when changing it so it will drain out more freely. Do a change every month or 1,000 miles, whichever comes first, for 3 months; that should reduce the sludge.

Pure and simple, the buildup of sludge is caused by the failure to follow the advice given in the owner's manual concerning how often to change the oil and filter. The best advice: religiously adhere to the maintenance schedule in your vehicle's owner's manual.

Oil and oil filters

Removing a stubborn oil filter

Getting the old filter off is sometimes the most difficult part of an oil change. Even if you have the right size filter wrench (you do, don't you?), there's never enough room for good leverage, and sometimes the filter seems to have become a part of the engine. Here are a few ways to deal with the reluctant critter:

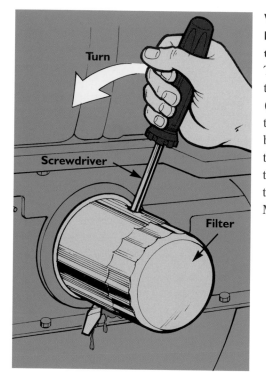

With a hammer, drive an large screwdriver through the lower half of the filter. Then turn the filter using the screwdriver as a lever. (Filters always loosen counterclockwise; you have been twisting in that direction, haven't you?) Remove the screwdriver and spin the filter off with your hand. Messy, but it works.

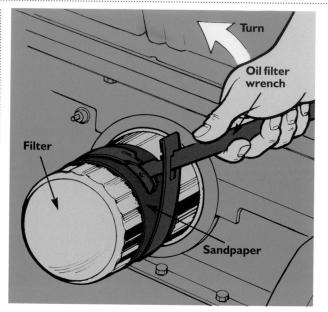

Sometimes your filter wrench just can't seem to get a grip on the filter housing. Well, give it some bite by wrapping coarse sandpaper around the filter (grit side against the filter) and then putting the wrench in place around the sandpaper.

Because you're not trying to preserve the filter, use any wrench or pliers that will get a grip on it. Very large slip-joint water pump pliers work well.

If you can get your hand up there but can't seem to get a grip, wear a rubber glove, or wrap a piece of sandpaper around the filter; or use one of those flat rubber gripper things from the kitchen drawer that you use to turn stuck jar lids.

As a last recourse, use a cold chisel and ball-peen hammer, positioning the chisel against the base of the filter. Work carefully so you don't damage the engine block, and wear safety goggles. ↓

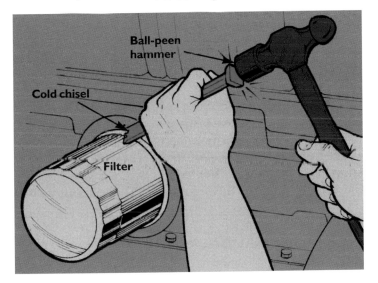

Ball-peen hammer

Cold chisel

Filter

Bob says . . .

Surviving a quickie oil change

Nowadays it seems as if there's a fast oil-change franchise on every busy corner. Many are very good. Unfortunately, they often rely on unskilled workers who are under pressure to turn things around fast, so you have to be careful. To make sure your quick oil change won't lead to other problems or end up costing you more than expected, keep these things in mind:

✔Call ahead and confirm that the shop has the correct oil and fluids in stock for your vehicle, and that only name-brand filters are used. Don't accept Brand X filters.

✔Make sure they use the correct type and **viscosity** of oil, as listed in your owner's manual.

✔Use only name brands of oil, and watch to make sure that what you asked for is what's actually installed.

✔Inform them if your 1995 or newer vehicle has Dex-Cool (orange) antifreeze (see p. 58).

✔Watch them work, rather than wandering into a waiting room and reading the newspaper—that keeps 'em honest.

✔Keep things simple. Don't authorize any work other than the oil change or such easy maintenance as a radiator flush/refill.

✔If your first impression is that the workers or business is disorganized, sloppy, or dirty, go elsewhere.

✔When they're done, review their work: Start the engine; get out and look for leaks at the oil filter. If no leaks are obvious, pull into the parking lot, stop the engine, and after a few minutes, check the oil level and any other fluid levels they checked.

Oil and oil filters

Troubleshooting high oil consumption

If your vehicle is using more than 2 quarts of engine oil in less than 2,000 miles, you need to take a careful look at the possible reasons. Check it out—if you delay, you could be looking at costly damage. First, be sure to check the oil with the car parked on level ground. Also, if the engine's been running, allow the oil to drain into the crankcase from the engine before pulling the dipstick. This takes 3 or 4 minutes. If you're checking the oil properly and you still think there's a problem with oil loss, use the charts here to help you investigate further. The chart below offers a quick summary of possible *causes*; the chart at right tackles the *solutions*.

If you delay in looking for the cause of an oil leak, you could end up looking at a big repair bill instead.

Driving conditions	Mechanical conditions	Other factors
Continuous high-speed driving	Piston rings not seated, or worn	Improper reading of dipstick
Towing a trailer or excess weight	Value guides and/or seals leaking	Improper grade or weight of oil
Excess idling	Failed/leaking engine gaskets or seals	Malfunctioning PCV system

Reasons for low oil level reading	Solution
Improper reading of dipstick	Make sure the vehicle is level, the oil has had time to drain into the oil pan, and the dipstick is fully seated into the tube.
Visible oil leaks	Look for oil spots under the vehicle for clues to the source. Tighten fasteners or replace leaky gaskets and seals. Install a new oil drain plug washer or new drain plug (see p. 40).
Improper oil viscosity (weight)	Your owner's manual has specific recommendations for your engine and climate. Follow them in choosing what oil to use.
Heavy use or high-speed driving	Pulling trailers or lengthy drives at high speeds will increase oil consumption—that's normal.
Crankcase ventilation or PCV system malfunction	Replace the PCV valve and hose, and clean the PCV vacuum port if necessary.
Piston rings of new or rebuilt engine not seated	New engines require a break-in period, typically 1,000 miles or more. Oil consumption will often be higher when the vehicle is new.
Broken or worn piston rings	You may see dark, oily smoke from the tailpipe, oil use will be high, and spark plugs may become oil-fouled. An expensive engine rebuild with new piston rings is the only cure.
Worn valve guides, valve stems, or valve seals	You may see blue smoke from the exhaust when starting the engine. Repair or rebuilding of cylinder heads is a costly but effective fix.

Heed the oil warning light

When the oil pressure warning light comes on, it means the engine has little or no oil pressure. If it lights while you're driving, shut the engine off immediately and check the oil level. If the warning light stays on for 5 or 6 seconds after you restart a car that's been sitting for several hours, the oil filter's check valve is leaking oil into the crankcase during off-engine periods. Replace the filter, and be sure the new one is right for your vehicle.

Dashboard warning lights are also called "idiot lights." Why? Because if you ignore them you're an idiot!

The oil-full truth about motor oil

Oil in your car's engine is unfit when it loads up with abrasives and metal particles, though this won't happen unless the engine is operated.

But even if a car is driven, say, 200 miles right after an oil change and then isn't driven for 3 months, the oil could still be contaminated. Oil also becomes unfit when additives in it weaken to the point where they no longer protect the engine against oxidation, rust, corrosion, sludge, and varnish. Although an engine may lie dormant, certain elements such as acid, moisture, and even air trapped inside the engine can affect the additives. That's why frequent oil changes are cheap insurance against engine problems whether the car is driven around a lot or not.

Too much of a good thing, however, can also lead to problems. Every so often a mechanic will add too much oil to your car's engine. How bad could that be?

Well, it's like putting too much detergent in your washing machine. All you get is suds, not clean clothes. Overfilling the engine causes bubbles to form in the oil, and air isn't much of a lubricant. Never overfill the **transmission** or the **differential**, either. Air can build up pressure inside the assembly, forcing lubricant to leak past gaskets and seals.

Oil and oil filters

Repairing a damaged drain plug

There you are, under your car, trying to save a few bucks by changing your own oil. You give the oil drain plug one last tug to make sure it's tight and—ARRGH!—you feel the threads strip. Now what?

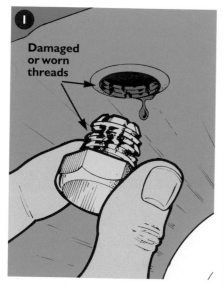

Damaged or worn threads

1. Take a close look at both the threads in the oil pan and on the plug. If only the plug is stripped, just buy a new one. But if the oil pan threads are damaged too, you need a special repair plug. Replacement and repair plugs are available from any auto parts store for a few dollars.

Oversize

Oversize with separate drain

Rubber plug

2. You'll find a variety of repair plugs on sale. The most common is simply an oversize plug, usually available in single and double oversize, that cuts new threads. There are also oversize versions that have a separate, smaller plug in the center that you loosen in order to drain the oil. Finally, there are a variety of rubber plugs that are a good choice if the oil pan threads are severely damaged.

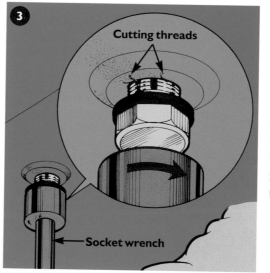

Cutting threads

Socket wrench

3. Install an oversize plug by first cleaning the damaged threads and then screwing in the new plug. Make sure it stays centered and perpendicular to the hole as you tighten it, or you'll damage the threads all over again.

Other fluids and filters

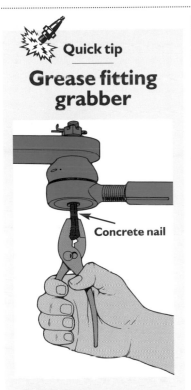
Remove a broken grease fitting by tapping a rectangular concrete nail into the remaining portion of the fitting, then twisting with pliers. It's painless, effective, and can be performed right on the vehicle.

Filter replacement guide

Your vehicles survive as long as they do, despite the conditions in which they have to operate, because a number of filters defend them. Replacing those filters at these recommended intervals, which may be more conservative than the manufacturer's specifications, remains your cheapest guarantee of trouble-free operation. The owner's manual for your vehicle is the best guide to replacement intervals, but if it's missing or you just need a little reminder, here's a guide to working with filters.

Filter	Function	Recommended replacement
Oil	Protects quality of engine oil by trapping and holding contaminants.	Every 3,000 to 4,000 miles with every oil change.
Air	Ensures clean air flow into carburetor or fuel injection system by trapping and holding dirt, dust, soot, and moisture.	Every 10,000 to 15,000 miles and with every tune-up.
Fuel	Removes contaminants from gasoline and diesel fuel before they enter carburetor, fuel injectors, and other parts.	Every 10,000 to 15,000 miles and with every tuneup.
Automatic transmission	Keeps transmission fluid clean, which is crucial for energy transfer, cooling, lubrication, and extended life.	Fluid and filter change every 12 months or 15,000 miles.
Breather element	Prevents harmful elements from entering engine.	Check at every oil change. Replace every 10,000 to 15,000 miles.
PCV filter	Helps keep the inside of the engine clean while reducing air pollution.	Check at every oil change. Replace every 10,000 to 15,000 miles.
Charcoal canister	Filters air used to purge the activated charcoal.	Every 15,000 miles and with every tune-up.
EGR valve solenoid	Traps impurities to keep EGR valve clean.	Every 15,000 miles and with every tune-up.

Other fluids and filters

When to replace transmission fluid

Automatic transmissions are complicated and expensive to repair. They require periodic filter and fluid changes just like the engine, and these are best done by the dealer rather than by a quickie oil change place. Your owner's manual has specific recommendations, but here are some tips on how to tell when it's time for a change, regardless of mileage.

1. Clear, pinkish red, or green (color varies by type used): When it looks like this, it's probably still OK.
2. Looks like a strawberry milkshake: You probably have a leak that's letting coolant to mix with transmission fluid. Get it fixed—the repair is inexpensive.
3. Dark reddish brown: If it has a burnt aroma and looks burnt, the fluid is overdue for a change.
4. Metal particles visible: Uh-oh! This is may be a sign of high wear and damage. Some metal debris is normal, so first get the fluid and filter changed right away. Drive a few thousand miles; then change fluid and filter again. If you still see debris, take the car to your dealer for an evaluation and possible overhaul.

Drip a few drops of the transmission fluid onto a clean white piece of paper towel. Here's what these spots will tell you:

Bob says . . .

Here's the skinny on brake fluid

Brake fluid can absorb moisture from the air, even if kept in a sealed container. Excess moisture turns brake fluid cloudy and lowers its boiling point. Accumulated moisture in a brake hydraulic system causes steel brake components to rust and rubber seals to swell and deteriorate, further contaminating this vital fluid. The result is a brake pedal that feels spongy or, worse, loss of braking power. Contaminants are bad news for antilock brake system pumps, motors, and solenoids.

Brake fluid is often the most overlooked safety item in a car. All major importers' maintenance schedules recommend flushing and replacing the brake fluid every 2 years or 30,000 miles. But for some unknown reason, domestic manufacturers don't include brake fluid flushing as part of their regularly scheduled maintenance. I disagree—I flush my car's system every 2 years or 30,000 miles.

Forgotten lube jobs

When you hear creaks and groans emerging from your vehicle as the shine and new-car smell begin to fade, it's time to lubricate some often forgotten moving parts.

Owners' manuals tell you a lot about major maintenance like oil changes but tend to ignore the little things that need regular attention. Here's a map of those forgotten spots:

1 Lithium grease
2 30-weight motor oil
3 Chassis grease
4 Graphite
5 Silicone spray
6 Silicone paste

Steer power

Lack of lubrication will kill a power-steering pump, rack, or gear. Power-steering hydraulic fluid, of course, is the medium that provides the power assist to steering. But it also lubricates the steering system.

Unless the reservoir is empty, you'll still have power steering. Low fluid level will often produce a loud whining/growling noise from the power-steering pump.

While checking the power-steering fluid level, place a few drops on a clean white paper rag or paper towel. Metal dust caused by a failed or failing part will cause the fluid to turn a silvery gray color. After repairs, flush the system with clean fluid.

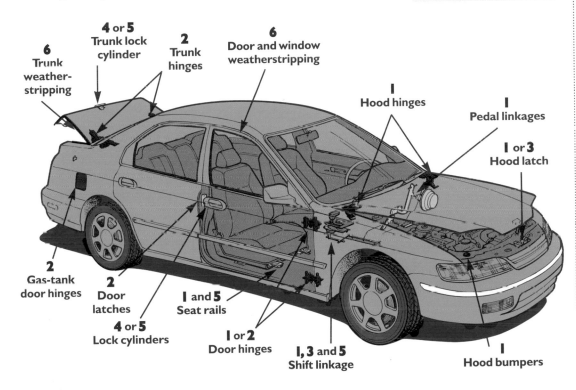

6 Trunk weather-stripping

4 or 5 Trunk lock cylinder

2 Trunk hinges

6 Door and window weatherstripping

I Hood hinges

I Pedal linkages

I or 3 Hood latch

2 Gas-tank door hinges

2 Door latches

4 or 5 Lock cylinders

I and 5 Seat rails

I or 2 Door hinges

I, 3 and 5 Shift linkage

I Hood bumpers

What a Gas!

You can forget to grease the joints or fill the windshield washers or even change the oil, but forget the fuel and you'll be hiking pretty quick. Probably in the rain . . . on the way to a meeting . . . with your boss in the car. Gasoline is one automobile fluid we all have to deal with regularly, whether we want to or not. And buying the stuff can take a sizable chunk out of even the most robust budget.

Yet despite the importance of fueling Ernest (or Wondertub or Ruby or whatever you call your four wheels), most people pretty much ignore gasoline except to gripe about the price. Well, the following pages prove that there's more to it than that. Many auto ailments can be traced to bad gas or the wrong kind of gas—even the wrong octane. Knowing what to buy and when to buy it can save money, too, and that's a fact anyone can appreciate.

Gasoline

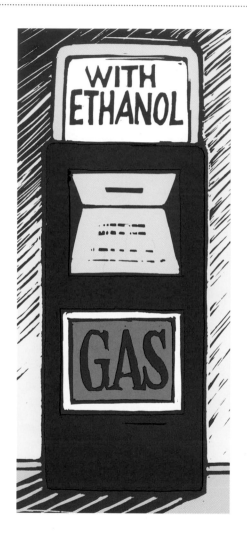

Don't fuel around when filling up

The era of full-service gas stations is long gone; these days it's a pump-it-yourself world. Although it's not difficult to fill a car with gas, there are a few simple precautions to keep in mind.

Always obey the NO SMOKING signs—getting blown deep into the next county isn't exactly how you want to get there.

As you drive into the station, try to orient the gas fill door so that it faces the pump. This is more than a convenience—snaking the pump's hose over your car can damage the paint. Turn the engine off before you get out of the car.

Gasoline is caustic, so if your skin is sensitive, keep some cheap latex gloves in the glove compartment. Remove the gas cap slowly so any pressure that has built up can dissipate harmlessly around the threads. You'll hear a hissing sound when this happens, particularly on hot days.

Keep your face away from the tank's inlet while filling the car, and try not to breathe any fumes that may escape—they smell terrible, and overexposure can make you sick.

Once the nozzle shuts off, just round off the cost of the gas—don't overfill the tank. Modern fuel tanks incorporate an air chamber to control fuel height and to contain vapors when the tank is being filled. Only 90% of the tank should be filled with gasoline; the remainder should be left empty to accommodate vapors when the gasoline expands.

When you finish fueling, replace the fuel filler cap and turn it until you hear several clicks. That's the signal that the cap is fully seated (a built-in **torque** limiter prevents the cap from being overtightened). If any gas spills on the car, don't rub it off—all you'll do is stain the paint. Instead, flush off any spilled gas with plenty of cool water as soon as you can.

Roadside fill-up

One of the worst experiences you can have on the road is running out of gas. If you belong to an automobile club and can find a public phone (or have a cellular phone), you can call for help and someone, eventually, will arrive with a couple of gallons for you. Then again, maybe you have a long hike ahead of you.

✔ Get the car as far off the road as you can.

✔ Use portable reflectors or emergency flashers to let oncoming motorists know that you have broken down. Don't use flares; they could ignite spilled fuel.

✔ Get just enough gas to get you started and back to the service station. A gallon of gas weighs about 7 pounds, so you don't want to lug more than you need back to the car. A gallon or so should do.

✔ Use only an approved, sealed container to transport gasoline back to the car.

✔ If you're traveling with someone else, one of you should keep an eye on traffic. That lets you pay attention to filling the tank.

✔ If your car is a fuel-injected model, pressurize the fuel system before trying to start the car: After the fuel cap is back in place,

Don't forget to check for reflectors and anything else you might have been using (especially the gas can!) before you drive away.

turn the ignition key to *On*, then to *Off* (without starting the car), two or three times. This will help the engine to start easier.

Why gas goes bad

For years, refiners processed crude oil into gasoline, added a few ounces of a lead-based antiknock compound, and delivered it to the service station. Times have changed. Leaded gas is no longer available for cars because of environmental concerns, among others. Problem is, plain gasoline evaporates during storage and as it does, harmful gum and varnish deposits can form in the tank. Gum, interacting with different metals in the fuel system (especially copper), causes the gas to turn rancid, or stale. Stale gas is cloudy and smells like paint thinner.

Refiners must now add a variety of detergents and stabilizers to keep gas fresh and to keep **fuel injectors** clean. Metal deactivators, rust inhibitors, and water dispersants are added to suppress the interaction between gas and metal in the fuel system. Oxidation inhibitors, such as phenols, prevent the formation of damaging gum deposits. In the winter, deicers are added to prevent gas line freeze-up. Lead? Who needs it!

 **Bob says . . .**

Don't use the wrong gas cap

If you lose a gas cap, find the right replacement or you could face serious problems. Caps on newer cars have a pressure-vacuum relief valve that's calibrated for the specific car. The valve opens when the pressure or vacuum in the fuel tank exceeds specifications. High pressure can cause poor drivability or make the tank and filters bulge. Fuel lines can leak or possibly blow off, creating a fire hazard. Too much vacuum can make the gas tank and lines collapse. So don't put just any old cap on—get the right one from an automotive parts supplier.

Gasoline

Octanes explained

Using a higher-**octane** fuel than your owner's manual calls for is a waste of money. The only major difference between two grades of fuel is the higher antiknock quality (octane) of premium. Buying gasoline that has a higher octane rating than your car needs provides absolutely no benefits. It doesn't produce more power or performance or fuel savings, contrary to advertising claims. Most of today's vehicles are designed to run just fine on 87-octane unleaded gas, called "regular"; check your owner's manual.

Premium fuel is not a better grade of fuel, nor does it contain more additives or detergents than regular gasoline. In fact, according to *Automotive Handbook*, the technical reference manual distributed by the Society of Automotive Engineers (SAE), the properties in gasoline that might

leave deposits which could affect the engine's valves are the same in type and quantity for both regular and premium gasoline.

Octane simply regulates combustion in the engine. You want the air/fuel mixture to meet the specs established by the automotive manufacturers—neither too lean nor too rich—because other-

wise valve damage can result. But that doesn't have diddly to do with octane number. The octane number is a measurement of the fuel's tendency not to knock.

The only time that unleaded premium might be necessary is if your vehicle suffers continual

The only one who benefits when you overbuy octane is the oil company.

engine knock at highway speeds (knock sounds like BB's ricocheting inside a metal pail). Light knocking is not a problem, however, and many cars will knock now and then.

If you'd like to read a more detailed analysis of gasoline, look at the January '90 issue of *Consumer Reports*. Check with the reference librarian at your library or order a back copy from Consumer Reports, P.O. Box 53016, Boulder, CO, U.S.A. 80322–3016.

Where's all the mileage?

If the mileage you're getting is even close to the estimates provided by government agencies, you're in good shape. Many people figure that those estimates are the minimum they should get, but in fact it's the other way around: your car will probably get poorer mileage than those laboratory estimates. Don't let anyone tell you otherwise just so they can sell you some replacement oxygen sensors (see p.81).

Fuel economy estimates for any car are exactly that: estimates for the not-very-real world. Mileage figures are calculated during controlled laboratory tests simulating urban road and highway driving conditions. The only purpose of the estimates is to help you compare the relative efficiency of different vehicles.

If you're really concerned about getting good mileage, one of the best things you can do is to check the tire pressure often and bring it up (or down) to specs. Make sure the engine is always tuned up, too. Mileage is also affected by:

✔ **Your driving habits:** Frequent short trips of less than 5 miles, especially when the temperature is below 65° F, result in extra fuel consumption because the engine never gets warm enough to work at its most efficient.

✔ **Dragging brakes:** Even a slight rubbing of the rotors or drums can cause fuel economy loss without producing excess heat or brake wear.

✔ **Parasitic loads:** Use of electrical devices (such as headlights or the rear-window defogger) will reduce fuel economy somewhat, but it's the air conditioner that's the thirstiest convenience.

✔ **Tires:** Tires that have a larger contact area (such as the high-performance 60 series tires) create more friction against the road, causing a car to use more gas than with narrower tires

✔ **Transmission:** Use overdrive if your car is equipped with this "extra" gear. Be sure the transmission is adjusted properly. A misadjusted **transmission** linkage will prevent the right information from being received by the car's engine computer. At highway speeds, this alone could result in a noticeable reduction in fuel efficiency.

✔ **Other factors:** You can lose mileage due to wind, road conditions, traffic levels, the number of passengers, terrain, and the gearing of your car. Even the air temperature can have something to do with it. In cold weather, for example, an engine will run rich (use more gas) until it warms up.

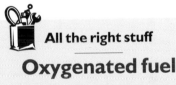

All the right stuff

Oxygenated fuel

As mandated by law, only oxygenated fuel may be sold in certain areas of the United States, to reduce pollution (in Canada it's widely available but not required). This gasoline contains a minimum of 2% oxygen and is blended to burn cleaner and evaporate more slowly, yet have no adverse effect on drivability or engine components. Oxygenated fuel does produce significantly less pollution than regular gasoline, but it isn't perfect: at present, it's a little more expensive and slightly reduces fuel economy.

Gasoline

Gas can cure cold-starting problems

If your fuel-injected car starts hard when cold and idles roughly, the problem might be related to the gas you're using. A manufacturer's advisory explains that "unless specified in the vehicle owner's manual," gasoline having an **octane** rating higher than 87 "is not required." Some people mistakenly use premium fuel when their manuals suggest regular, thinking that primo stuff is better able to keep **fuel injectors** clean. Not true.

It is true, however, that the brand of gasoline may contribute to cold-engine performance problems. So why not switch to a different brand—and use regular, not premium—for a couple of tankfuls to see if there's any improvement.

Although octane regulates combustion, correct fuel *volatility* is responsible for cold-weather starting, warm-up, and drivability. Volatility is the gasoline's ability to change from a liquid to a vapor.

The **combustion chamber** temperature may rise to 1500° F when an engine is warm, but before start-up on a cold morning, the combustion chamber temperature may be zero. For fuel to burn properly in hot *and* cold temperatures, it has to include a combination of ingredients that can vaporize at various temperatures. Each refiner uses slightly different ingredients; that's what makes one gas different from another.

The amount of carbon residue left behind after gas burns depends on the quality and the volatility of the gasoline being used. Today's highly sophisticated engines need high-quality and high-volatility fuels to minimize carbon buildup.

If changing to a different brand of gas doesn't improve cold-weather starting problems, however, you may be dealing with another fuel-related problem. Some cars have cold-engine starting trouble as a result of oxygenated gasoline, which is sold in many states during the winter to reduce the higher emissions produced during cold weather. If your starting problems don't seem to be related to oxygenated gasoline, get your service technician on the case. A good one will check for these likely causes:

✔ Faulty **MAP sensor**

✔ Faulty **idle air control**

✔ Sticking **EGR valve**

✔ Contaminated **oxygen sensor**

✔ Leaking **fuel pressure regulator** hose

✔ Malfunctioning **TPS switch**

According to a U.S. consumer group called Public Citizen, car owners waste billions of dollars annually by needlessly purchasing high-octane gasoline. All grades and brands of gasoline contain detergents to help keep fuel injectors clean. If this is the reason you're buying premium, you're just wasting your money.

 Bob says . . .

Look out for carbums

Carbon might make great diamonds, but I hate to see it in a car. A product of incomplete combustion, it can build up in the engine's air intake housing or on the throttle plate, and the symptoms mimic those of a vacuum leak or a bad **TPS** signal. Your car's onboard computer will mistakenly figure that the throttle plate is open and will probably change the fuel delivery and spark timing to compensate; it might even open the **EGR valve**. A shady mechanic will try to sell you an expensive repair, but here's the real fix: use throttle body and air intake cleaner to remove carbon, gum, and varnish buildup inside the housing.

Rx for fuel injectors

Instead of a carburetor, most newer cars contain **fuel injectors**. If they're not operating properly, they can cause an engine to run and idle roughly. The trick is having your mechanic decide if they're clogged or if they're defective mechanically or electrically. If they're clogged, you might be able to clean them.

✔ Try adding a container or two of fuel injector cleaner to the gas tank. There are many good brands out there, and your local parts supplier should be able to recommend one.

✔ High-pressure fuel injector cleaning is generally OK for older vehicles. The injectors on almost all newer makes ('88 and up), however, can be damaged by harsh high-pressure cleaning.

✔ A relatively new ultrasonic cleaning process uses a special calibration fluid. The fluid, vibrating at high frequency, loosens any microscopic particulates. The injectors are then cycled on and off to wash out any deposits.

If a fuel injector cleaning or additive doesn't help, one or more injectors are damaged and must be replaced. But just because one injector is bad, there's no reason to replace all of the other ones.

The problem of clogged fuel injectors prevailed in the days when fuel-injection systems were relatively rare. But no longer. All brands of gas, as well as all grades from regular to premium, contain detergent that neutralizes contaminants before they can clog the injectors. A clog prevents a full spray of fuel from reaching the **combustion chamber** and leads to hard starting, stalling, and hesitation.

One last thing: Have a new fuel filter installed before the injectors clog. It's your fuel injectors' lone defense against contaminants.

Gasoline

Gas cap whooosh

If you feel as if you're fueling a time bomb every time a rush of air escapes past the gas cap you just loosened, calm down. The pressure buildup is normal and harmless.

Gasoline vapor expands and contracts with changes in temperature. It's usually kept from escaping into the atmosphere (and causing pollution), but the vapors have to go somewhere, so they're routed to a charcoal canister.

If you're in the habit of running the tank nearly dry before refilling it, the amount of vapor will be greater than if you had refueled earlier. The vapors are contained in an air chamber, so get out of the practice of topping off the tank. When you overfill it, the vapors have nowhere to collect. Furthermore, if the car heats up quickly, as it would if you drove it from a cool garage into the hot sun, the amount of vapor will be even greater. It could be so great, in fact, that the line conducting it

Relax. Even though your gas tank may feel pressured, you shouldn't be.

onto the charcoal canister would not be able to handle it. The result will be some pressurization of the tank, and if that's when you remove the gas cap, you'll hear the rush of pressure being released.

So you're safe, and the tank is not about to explode. The gas cap has a built-in relief valve that opens and vents the tank if the pressure gets too great. If the rush of air still concerns you, you can probably prevent it by filling the tank in the morning when the temperature is cooler, and by opening the gas cap slowly to let the pressure release gradually.

Stopping minor gas tank leaks

A leaking gas tank will quickly become obvious. If it's a minor leak, usually along one of the metal flanges, you can fix it quickly for under $20. Repair or replacement by a service shop would cost from $80 to several hundred dollars, so this quick, cheap fix is worth trying.

1. Drive around until the tank is nearly empty; try to get the fuel level below the leak. Stop at your auto parts store and purchase one of the two-part epoxy gas tank repair kits and a spray can of brake parts cleaner, which is a strong solvent. When the fuel level is low enough, begin your repair by thoroughly cleaning the area around the leak with the brake cleaner. Wear rubber gloves and eye protection. Clean a 6- to 8-square-inch area around the leak.

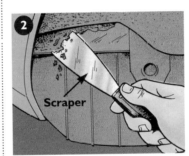

2. Scrape and then sandpaper away any road tar, undercoating, rustproofing, rust, or baked-on grime from around the leak. Rust and dirt will prevent the epoxy from successfully sealing the leak. Once the area is scraped clean, flush it again with the brake cleaner and let it dry.

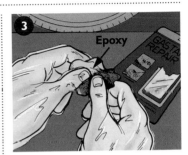

3. Cut off equal amounts from the two epoxy sticks, wearing clean plastic gloves. Peel away any wrapping, and knead the material between your fingers until it is one uniform color.

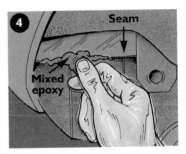

4. Roll the epoxy into a cone shape, and push it firmly into the hole, or into the leaky flange or seam. Smooth out the excess with a plastic spreader, and allow the epoxy to cure completely.

Other fuels

All about gasohol

In recent years, some refiners have been blending ethanol and methanol with gasoline. These substances keep fuel systems clean, enhance the octane, and lower emissions at the tailpipe. Even better, blended gasoline can reduce the cost of a fill-up. Fuels that contain ethanol or methanol are called gasohol.

Ethanol, an alcohol made from a grain product such as corn, alfalfa, or soybeans, is also called "ethyl" or "grain" alcohol. It works like a deicing additive to keep ice from forming in the fuel system. Most cars can safely use a blend of 10% ethanol and 90% unleaded gasoline.

Methanol, which can be made from wood, coal, or even garbage, is often referred to as "methyl" or "wood" alcohol. Most cars can safely use a blend of 5% methanol, 93% unleaded gasoline, and 2% cosolvent (an ingredient that keeps methanol and gasoline from separating and prevents corrosion

damage to fuel system parts). Excessive amounts of methanol or the absence of a cosolvent can corrode metal parts in the fuel system and can damage plastic and rubber parts.

Because ethanol vaporizes at a lower temperature than gasoline, it can lead to drivability problems such as vapor lock, hesitation, and stumble. If your car develops any of these conditions, switch back to straight gasoline.

Since the late 1980's, all fuel systems are compatible with gasohol, provided the fuel meets guidelines set by the vehicle's manufacturer (check the owner's manual). In fact, the solvent action of alcohol can prevent deposits from forming in the fuel system. The bad news is that this same characteristic can quickly plug fuel filters in older cars by breaking loose any accumulated sludge and varnish, attacking the lead/tin coating of the gas tank, and freeing up rust from inside the tank and fuel lines.

Natural gas pros and cons

Alternative fuels such as compressed natural gas (CNG) offer several advantages over gasoline but have significant disadvantages, too.

CNG is less expensive than gasoline, yet it offers similar mileage. It's the least polluting fuel, and burns so clean that oil changes need be done only every 12,000 miles; spark plugs should last 75,000 miles.

But converting to CNG is costly. The entire fuel system, including the fuel tank, will have to be replaced. CNG tanks (cylinders) can weigh 300 pounds even when empty, and the fuel has a higher ignition temperature and evaporates quicker.

There's plenty of CNG in North America, but very little commercial infrastructure to provide convenient refueling. You could pump natural gas from your home's gas system, but you'll need an expensive compressor to do it and a lot of time: a 1-cfm compressor takes 3 to 5 hours to fill a tank that's completely empty.

Bob says . . .
Get the good stuff!

It's very important to buy gasohol from a reputable dealer. Don't hesitate to ask about the blend percentage, how often it's tested, and how fresh it is. Look for a filter on the pump that will protect your car against contaminants. Some states (though no provinces) require a label on the pump that specifies the percentage of alcohol in the mixture; if there's no label, buy your fuel elsewhere.

Water in diesel fuel

Water collecting in the fuel tank of diesel-powered vehicles has always been a particular problem. Compression in a diesel engine can be as high as 22:1, but because water doesn't compress, serious engine damage is likely if too much water ends up in the combustion chamber. To warn of water in the engine and fuel system, diesel cars are usually equipped with a "water-in-fuel" dashboard warning light.

Where does the water come from? Not from the engine, as some people think. Rather, it's probably from your fuel source. The water could be from condensation in the fuel storage tanks or from groundwater seepage, but whatever the source it does no good if it winds up in the fuel tank of your car.

So what to do? Well, start by going to service stations that cater to 18-wheelers (you can usually find them near major highways). These places sell a lot of diesel and it'll be fresh and—hopefully—free of water. You can also purchase an optional external fuel filter that has a built-in water separator. They were fairly common during the early 1980's, when there were lots of diesel passenger vehicles. The add-on filter lets you easily drain accumulated water every week or two via a petcock valve. A repair shop that specializes in truck repairs and service can probably help you locate such a filter.

But don't wait for the car's warning light to come on before you do something about a recurring water problem—it's better to take some preventive steps. First, try another fuel source. If changing suppliers doesn't resolve things, have the add-on water separater installed. If you can't find a separator, your only remaining option is an annoying one: you'll have to drain the water from the car's fuel filter every few weeks. The extra effort, though, will pay off in smooth performance.

Whenever an antique car passes by, do you find yourself wondering what driving was like back when good roads (and good maps) were few? Yep, car travel back then was an adventure, not just another way to get to work or transport groceries. In those days, motorists got to experience Mom Nature firsthand. Heat was whatever radiated up from the engine, and air conditioning was something that hadn't yet arrived in buildings, let alone vehicles.

These days, though, controlled heating and cooling, both for you and for the engine, are crucial parts of an enjoyable drive. Of all the Big Uh-Ohs of automotive life, overheating is among the most annoying, not to mention potentially the biggest wallet shredder.* Here's the inside story on how you and your engine can beat the weather and head off expensive problems.

*Some other Big Uh-Ohs: Roaring past a radar cop, losing your keys, and getting your tie caught in the fan belt . . .

Radiator and coolant

Engine coolant: Which is which

Most car manufacturers recommend flushing and refilling the cooling system with new **coolant** every 2 years or 24,000 miles. You're really pushing it if you leave the old stuff in any longer. Although the freeze protection will stay the same, the coolant's anticorrosive and lubricating additives will be worn out. Excessive corrosion can damage the radiator, clog the heater core, ruin the thermostat, and cause the **water pump** to fail. Even worse is the internal engine damage that could occur. Most new car engine blocks, heads, intake manifolds, and internal coolant sealing gaskets are made of metal alloys. When antifreeze breaks down, corrosive acids attacks these parts. The result is premature engine failure caused by internal coolant leaks you can't even see. You might not see drops on the driveway, but you might notice that the coolant overflow bottle is always empty. Replacing the coolant is cheap insurance, just like regular oil changes.

The cooling system is designed to maintain the correct engine operating temperature, and that's what prevents premature wear of the crankshaft and engine bearings. Coolant temperature is one of the first pieces of information the **electronic control unit** looks at, and if the temperature is off, the ECU may adjust other factors for good drivability. An engine running at its proper temperature will run better and cleaner.

A few other coolant pointers:

1. Don't use recycled coolant. While some manufacturers have given a limited OK to specific recycled products, standard coolant is cheap enough that you shouldn't hesitate to use it when it comes time to flush your system.

2. Some manufacturers have approved relatively new propylene-based coolants that are supposed to be more environmentally friendly than regular coolant. But propylene glycol has a higher **viscosity** than ethylene glycol and may result in poorer performance by the defroster and heater. It also boils over at a lower

> **Replacing coolant is cheap insurance, just like getting a regular oil change. Be sure to get the right stuff.**

temperature than ethylene glycol and freezes at a higher temperature. These products may not be approved by *all* auto manufacturers, and cost more too. Make sure your car's warranty won't be voided by using them.

3. Dex-Cool is the latest in coolant and antifreeze technology. It's an extended-life engine coolant that has been used in all General Motors vehicles since about mid-'95. It has a service change interval of 5 years/100,000 miles, whichever comes first. That's more than twice the standard coolant change interval. The bright orange color of Dex-Cool distinguishes it from other coolants, and for good reason.

If old-style coolant somehow gets mixed with Dex-Cool in the first 3,000 miles, the system has to be completely drained and refilled. Even a few drops can contaminate the coolant (remember that quick-change oil shops often top off the coolant as part of their service, so warn them not to contaminate the Dex-Cool).

4. No matter what type of antifreeze you use, the mixing percentage is easy to remember. A 50:50 mixture (1 part antifreeze to 1 part water) is what the manufacturers recommend.

Working safely beneath a car

Changing the **coolant** in most new cars can be extremely difficult because the **petcock** (beneath the radiator) may be recessed. You might have to use pliers to loosen it, though using your fingers is best. Even getting at the petcock can be tricky—you can't reach down through the engine compartment, and on low-slung cars there won't be enough clearance to let you shinny under there. You'll probably have to raise the front wheels to reach the petcock.

Working under a raised car is a task that cries out for caution. Unless a car is securely supported, don't get under it. Use drive-on ramps (or jack stands) and wheel chocks. You can make a chock— you'll need two of them—by cutting one end of a 2x4 wood block to a 45° angle. After driving onto ramps or placing jack stands under the front of the car, push the mitered end of each chock under the rear

SO WHAT DID YA DO WID DA COOLANT?!

> **Working under a car is a task that cries out for caution. Be certain that the car is secure.**

of each back tire. Then place an automatic **transmission** in *Park*, a manual transmission in gear, and make sure the parking brake is fully engaged no matter what type of transmission is involved.

As it drains, catch the coolant in a pail or large pan—don't let it seep into the soil to contaminate the groundwater. And whether you're on a city sewer service or using a septic system, never pour the coolant into a drain. Instead, pour the stuff from the pail or pan into 64-ounce juice bottles or plastic containers. Used coolant can be considered a hazardous waste, so take the containers to a local shop that recycles coolant; there may be a slight charge for disposal. The other alternative is to store the coolant out of harm's way (particularly out of a child's reach) until your community holds a hazardous waste disposal day.

Radiator and coolant

Coolant keeps you going

There's nothing especially complex about the cooling system. A yearly checkup isn't difficult, doesn't take long, and can save you from expensive repairs. Do these checks with the engine cold. Start with the **radiator** cap. Remove it by twisting it while pushing down, as you would with a childproof bottle. If it refuses to budge, careful use of slip-joint pliers may be necessary.

1. Check the coolant. Test the **coolant** to determine its freezing point, using a hydrometer from any auto parts store. (Spend a few more dollars to get a good one. The best use a graduated float; the less expensive rely on a floating ball.) Add coolant and water to adjust the freezing point to a level that assumes the worst about your area's winter weather.

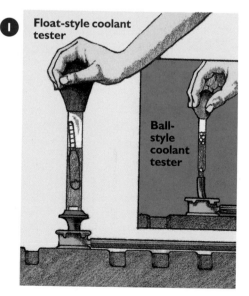

① Float-style coolant tester

Ball-style coolant tester

②

Worn, cracked, or missing seal

2. Inspect the cap. Although inexpensive, the radiator cap is an important part of the cooling system. Make sure that the rubber seals are clean, pliable, complete, and uncracked. If the cap looks worn or fits poorly, replace it with one that's specifically designed for your car model.

3. Look inside. Check and clean the radiator neck (where the cap attaches). With a flashlight, look at the coolant inside the radiator. If rust or other contamination is visible, it's time to replace the coolant. If the radiator core (the passages inside the radiator) is partially plugged, have the system back-flushed. If there's oil present, the engine has an internal leak and requires professional attention. If you suspect a leak, start the engine and shine your flashlight into the neck. If you see bubbles, there's an internal leak and you'd best get your car to a mechanic.

③

Rust

Radiator core

Radiator neck

Overheating primer

Whether your car is new or old, pinpointing a persistent overheating problem can be difficult, and many mechanics are too quick to change parts without troubleshooting. Here's what they should be looking for:

✔ Clogged fins on the **radiator** or air-conditioner condenser. Flush debris with a hose, working from the back side of the radiator.

✔ Improper **coolant** mix.

✔ Loose fan belt. The fan can't cool if it isn't turning.

✔ Loss of cooling system pressure due to a leak or a faulty radiator cap.

✔ Poor coolant circulation. With the engine warm and idling at 2,000 RPM, peer into the radiator to see if the coolant is bubbling with vigor. If it's not, either a weak **water pump** or a faulty **thermostat** is the likely culprit.

✔ A partially stuck thermostat (see p.64).

✔ Clogged radiator tubes. Blockages that restrict the flow of coolant are a common cause of overheating, especially in older vehicles. If chemical cleaning and back-flushing fails to clear the blockage, have the radiator removed and tested. It may be possible to salvage the old one with a chemical flush and rodding.

✔ A failed thermostatic clutch. This clutch limits the fan speed to help an engine reach operating temperature quickly. As the temperature rises, the clutch backs off to let the fan reach full speed.

✔ Faulty high-speed electric cooling fan. Check for an electrical malfunction.

✔ Air trapped in the cooling system. Have the air purged, a task which involves loosening an air-bleed screw on the thermostat housing, running the engine at idle speed, and adding coolant until it flows from the air-bleed hole.

✔ Pinched-off coolant recovery reservoir hose. Unkink it.

✔ Wrong size fan. If your engine has a five-blade fan, consider switching to a seven-blade fan or installing an auxiliary fan to provide greater air circulation.

✔ Faulty temperature-sending unit or temperature gauge or warning light. Perhaps the engine isn't really overheating— check for false signals given by faulty parts.

Heat checks

Here's what to check if your car overheats at highway speeds:

Has the front air deflector fallen off? It diverts air over the radiator to assist in cooling. Look at the lower radiator hose (at the outlet end of the radiator). There's a spring inside to keep the hose from collapsing during vacuums created at high engine speeds. If the spring collapses, coolant won't get anywhere. Have a mechanic check the ignition timing. By itself, faulty timing won't usually cause an engine to overheat, but it can make the temperature higher than it should be.

 **Bob says . . .**

You did WHAT?

The most frustrating overheating problem I ever encountered involved a car that had been in a front-end accident. The body shop repairing it had installed a new fan . . . with the blades facing backward! The car was overheating fresh out of the shop because very little air was being pulled through the radiator.

Radiator and coolant

Mysterious coolant loss

One of the most annoying things about owning a car is trying to track down a mysterious, invisible **coolant** leak. One symptom: the level in the coolant recovery tank drops below the *Full Cold* mark when the engine is warm, rather than rising to the *Full Hot* mark as it should. No tell-tale leaks under the car, the car runs fine...but you keep adding coolant anyway. A bit of evaporation could account for some of it, but coolant shouldn't disappear at a high rate out of a system that is sealed (except for the vented recovery tank).

If you've given up on finding the source of the leak, have your repair facility pressure-test the cooling system. Two areas to look at would be the head gasket and the **transmission** oil cooler. The motor oil and transmission fluid should be clear. If coolant is leaking past the **head gasket**, the motor oil will turn a caramel color. If the transmission cooler (located in the radiator) is leaking, the fluid will be the color of a strawberry milkshake.

There are five other possible causes for this problem:

1. The cooling system isn't being filled correctly. Begin with a stone-cold engine. Remove the radiator cap and fill the radiator to the brink with **antifreeze** and water (you want a 50:50 mix). Reinstall the cap so that any marks on it, such as arrows, line up with marks on the radiator—that's how you'll know that the cap is on tight. Finally, remove the cap from the coolant recovery tank and fill the tank to the *Full Cold* mark with the same mix of antifreeze and water.

2. There's something wrong with the radiator cap. Manufacturers recommend that you replace the cap periodically; have it inspected during regular servicing and pressure-tested every 2 years. If the cap doesn't hold pressure, or if it looks damaged, replace it—a new one is cheap. When installing a new cap, coat the rubber seals and gaskets with fresh antifreeze. Make sure the replacement meets manufacturer specifications.

YOU DON'T NEED A COAT, SON— ONLY PEOPLE ARE AFFECTED BY WINDCHILL!

ANTIFREEZE

3. The coolant recovery system has a leak. Have the tank and hoses removed and checked for leaks, especially along any seams in the tank.

4. A sneaky leak. One place would be in a heater return hose where the hose passes over the **exhaust manifold**. The hose will leak only when the engine is running and the heater is on. A pressure test of the cooling system won't pinpoint the leak because the test is made with the engine and heater turned off. No sign of coolant is left on the engine, either, because as the drops leak from the hose they fall on the hot exhaust manifold and burn away. Now that's a *really* sneaky leak. So if nothing else checks out as the problem, tell your mechanic to check out the heater.

5. Maybe it's the water pump. Many **water pumps** have a small weep hole in their design that allows seepage if the housing's ceramic seal is starting to leak. Thermal shock (adding cold water to a hot engine) and abrasives in worn-out coolant can damage the seal or mar the pump bearing shaft, allowing a loss of coolant. The seepage will be even greater if the cooling system has been overfilled.

Easy hose replacement

The best time to replace a cooling system hose is before it fails. That way you'll be working with a cool engine, the right tools, the correct hose, a minimal loss of coolant, and the least distraction.

The worst time for replacement is while you're stranded beside a highway.

Finding a replacement hose can be a hassle. First call nearby auto parts stores and see if they have the hose you need in stock. Lower **radiator** hoses are reinforced with internal springs to help them maintain their shape; upper hoses with pleats are easier to work with. When purchasing any hose, get new worm-drive hose clamps as well. And don't forget that **coolant** is both poisonous and sweet-tasting: Keep children and pets away as you let the coolant drain into a pan.

Check the hoses, including those for the heater, every 6 months. They're candidates for replacement if they are cracked, leaking, oil-soaked, or if they feel unusually hard or spongy when squeezed. Even if they look fine, replace them if they're more than 2 years old. Here's how:

1. If the old hose won't slide off, slit it with a utility knife and peel it off the radiator neck. Never pry or pound away at a stuck hose. The radiator neck is delicate and is easily damaged.

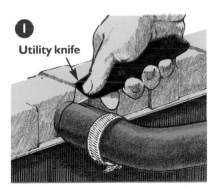

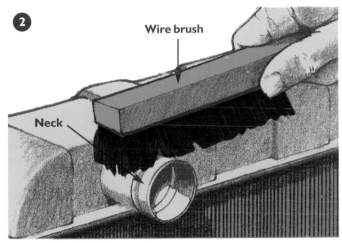

2. Clean off the radiator neck with a wire brush before attaching the new hose.

3. Dip the hose ends in coolant so they'll slide on easier. Slide both new hose clamps onto the hose and then install the hose. Position the hose clamps so they're just to one side of the ridge on the necks, and then tighten. Place the clamps so that the screwhead is easy to get at.

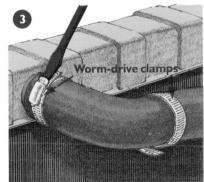

Radiator and coolant

Is your 'stat working properly?

There are a number of things that will cause inaccurate readings on your engine temperature gauge. One of the most common is a sticky **thermostat**, but it's easy to find out if your thermostat is working properly. Drive the car for about 20 minutes. Then turn on the heater, switch the blower to high speed, and hold your hand under the heater duct. If little or no hot air blows from the duct, the thermostat is stuck in the open position and is keeping the engine from reaching its normal operating temperature. Another way to test this is to pull the car over, lift the hood, and feel the upper **radiator** hose; it should be hot after a 20-minute drive. Install a new thermostat to correct the problem.

If the thermostat turns out to be OK, however, a little more investigation is called for. Your mechanic should use an electrical tester to determine whether any of the following items is at fault:

✔ The temperature-sending unit can sometimes fail.

✔ A loose or corroded wire can play havoc with signals that should be zipping smoothly between the sending unit and the temperature gauge.

✔ Maybe there's trouble with the instrument cluster's circuit board.

✔ And if the temperature gauge needle barely lifts itself off the lowest reading, even after you've been out for a nice little spin, maybe the gauge itself has given up the ghost.

Replacing a thermostat

Changing your car's **thermostat** every 2 years is easy, inexpensive ($10 to $20 at auto parts stores), and helps guard against a host of problems. At the same time, back-flush the system and replace the old **coolant** and any aging hoses. Here's how to replace the thermostat.

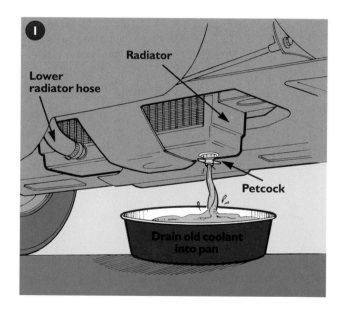

Radiator

Lower radiator hose

Petcock

Drain old coolant into pan

1. Open the radiator drain fitting (petcock) that's usually on the bottom of the radiator. Let the coolant drain into a container, and then dispose of it in a proper fashion; never dump it out on the ground or into a drain (see p.59). Coolant is poisonous, so don't let it sit around. While the radiator is draining, inspect the radiator hoses and replace any that look questionable or feel stiff and brittle.

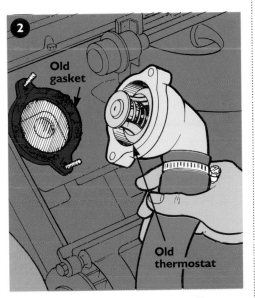

Old gasket

Old thermostat

2. Remove the upper radiator hose (loosen the hose clamp) and unbolt the thermostat cover. Carefully separate the **thermostat** cover from the engine — a few light taps might be necessary, but never pry it off. Scrape the old gasket off with a putty knife, and polish the metal surfaces and bolts with steel wool. You want everything clean and corrosion-free.

3. Install the new thermostat in its cover, with the spring side facing out. Coat the new gasket with a thin film of automotive sealer and put it in place on the engine.

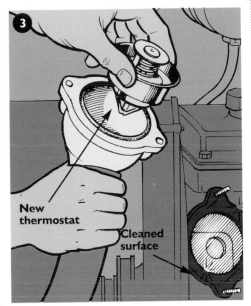

New thermostat

Cleaned surface

4. Seat the cover over the gasket and bolt it down. Reattach the upper radiator hose.

5. Close the petcock; refill the system with a 50:50 mix of antifreeze and water (or as recommended in your owner's manual). Never exceed a 70:30 ratio. Start the engine and check for leaks.

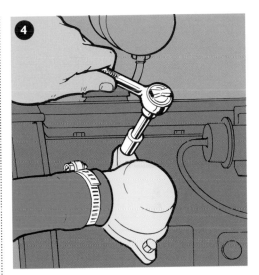

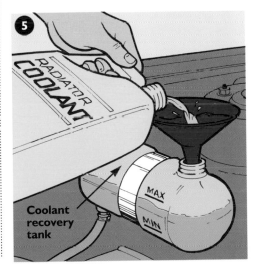

RADIATOR COOLANT

MAX

MIN

Coolant recovery tank

Radiators and coolant

Water pump failure

The **water pump** is the heart of the cooling system. It forces coolant through the engine block, heater core, and **radiator**. If you're experiencing pump failure on a newer car, take it to the dealer to find out what's wrong.

The dealer may be overreacting if he replaces the pump just because there's a bit of seepage from the weep hole. Some people might interpret this minor coolant loss as a sign of water pump failure, but it's normal.

However, if the discharge is significant, it means the pump seal is breaking down for one of the following reasons:

✔ Abrasives in old **coolant** will cause the seal and bearing to wear out. This is yet another argument (if you still needed to hear one) for keeping your coolant fresh, fresh, fresh.

✔ The belt that drives the water pump can be too tight. Have the dealer check whether the drive belt itself is too tight, or whether it's the self-adjuster (tensioner) that's overly eager.

✔ Heavy-duty radiator cleaners can damage the pump seal. Don't use these products.

✔ The coolant may have too much ethylene glycol (**antifreeze**) and not enough water, and that can cause the water pump seal to swell or crack.

In most cases the coolant mixture should be 50:50 water and ethylene glycol.

✔ Hard water in some parts of the country contains minerals that can cause seal failure.

✔ A cracked, bent, or even an out-of-balance fan blade will cause problems.

✔ A worn fan clutch.

✔ Adding cold water to a hot engine (thermal shock).

✔ A defective **thermostat** that allows the coolant to aerate. This lowers the pump's efficiency and causes wear and rusting at three times the normal rate.

LOOKS LIKE YOU NEED A NEW WATER PUMP!

AGAIN!?

 **In the know**

Got a better method?

Freeze plugs, core plugs, expansion plugs, whatever you call them, they don't "pop out" to prevent the block from cracking if your engine freezes. Instead, they simply plug holes left during a manufacturing process called sand casting: the holes drain sand from the engine block after casting.

Air-conditioning systems

AC system checkup

Modern automotive air-conditioning (AC) systems are virtually maintenance-free, efficient, reliable, sealed, and (since 1995) environmentally friendly. But they can, and do, fail. Here's how to keep cool.

Test it yourself. No special tools or equipment is needed. With the engine warmed up and running, set the fan on *High,* move the temperature control to *Cold,* and turn on the air conditioning.

Did the engine slow as the compressor engaged? It should have. Don't be concerned, however, if the compressor cycles on and off regularly—it's normal for many late-model cars.

Once the system has stabilized after several minutes of operation, sense the temperature of the air blowing from the vents with the back of your hand. Is it cold? Depending on the outside ambient temperature, humidity, and sun load, it should be about 50° F. If you're not sure, stick a thermometer into the vent and read the actual temperature.

If the system is working normally and the air is cold, here is another thing you can check on your own. With the engine off and cold, inspect the rubber drive belt that powers the AC compressor. Check the tension by pushing down with your thumb at the center of the belt's longest span. It should have ½ inch of play. Be wary of repeatedly adjusted V-belts; they narrow as they wear. Replace worn, cracked, or frayed belts before they fail.

Here's one last check you can make. Open the hood, turn on the car, and then turn on the air conditioner. After a while, the cooling fan should turn on. If it doesn't, there might be a problem with the engine temperature sensors, the ECU, the air-conditioning control switch, or the air-conditioning pressure switches; all are involved in turning on the fan to draw air through the air conditioner's condenser.

When you've done all you can do. If the air coming from the vents is cool, not cold, it's likely that the system has lost some of its **refrigerant**—Freon, as it's known. And if the compressor failed to engage or delivered only warm air during your initial test, it's likely that the system is completely discharged. Some systems include pressure switches that are designed to bleed off excess pressure. If the switches opened, they probably did so to protect the compressor. This indicates that there's a serious problem in the system somewhere; call in a professional to find out what's going on. Once he or she locates and repairs the leak, the system will have to be evacuated, relubricated, and recharged.

Evaporator

Older air conditioning systems may have pressure-test valves on portions of the line. These valves look like tire-pressure valves, but they should only be handled by professionals using special test equipment. This is not a do-it-yourself job!

Compressor

Condenser

Receiver/dryer

Air-conditioning systems

Detecting an AC leak

One of the most difficult problems to locate on a car is a Freon leak. This isn't a do-it-yourself project, either. The old standby of leak detection—a dash of soapy water brushed onto the fittings—won't work in this case. That's because if the leak is bad enough to bubble the soap, it's bad enough to bleed off the Freon entirely before you even get a chance to investigate the problem.

Instead of soap, automobile repair professionals use special dyes and sophisticated electronic leak detectors. But the savviest mechanics know that there's sometimes another way to spot signs of a Freon leak, and to use this method all you need is good eyesight.

Refrigerant oil is carried along with the Freon throughout the air-conditioning system; its job is to lubricate the compressor. The oil naturally leaks out along with the Freon, and dirt clings to it. Look for an accumulation of oily dirt around the AC fittings, compressor, hoses, and lines; also look for oily residue stains seeping down the condenser. Tightening the hose fittings may stop the leak. Also, you might want to check the evaporator core—see if there's a buildup of dirt on the core. But a mechanic should never rely solely on visual inspection to check leaks; electronic leak detectors will find what the eye cannot. Once the leak is gone, the air-conditioning system must be recharged.

> **Tracking a leak can drive you crazy—your best bet is to find a pro to find the leak.**

Goodbye to Freon

In the spring, the air-conditioning system of many cars may have to be recharged in order to replenish the Freon (R-12) lost over the winter. Usually the Freon leaks past the compressor's ceramic seal or hose connector O-rings. In the old days you could recharge the system yourself for a few dollars. These days, however, Freon is worth its weight in gold.

As of January 1, 1996, it is illegal to produce R-12 **refrigerant** in the United States and Canada, and illegal to import it. But there are millions of cars still on the road that were built before 1994, and they use R-12 in their AC systems. If this describes your car, here's what you can do if your air conditioner fails:

1. Fix the system and reinstall R-12. That's a sound choice as long as R-12 is available. How long that will be, however, is anyone's guess.

2. Retrofit the system to R-134a, the non-CFC refrigerant used in all post-1995 vehicles, or another refrigerant recommended by the dealer. According to GM, only the component that fails has to be replaced. The system should then be flushed using a special solvent that removes any gunk that may remain. The correct amount of a new type of AC refrigerant oil (PAG oil) will have to be added, new service valves installed, and the system evacuated of all air and moisture. Systems retrofitted with R-134a are filled to 90% of the capacity of the old R-12. A rule of thumb good mechanics go by: Replace the **receiver dryer/accumulator** if the system has been opened to the atmosphere (left unsealed) for an extended period.

3. Use one of the new and less-hazardous products, such as FR-12. This compatible refrigerant can be installed easily in an operational R-12 air-conditioning system. Only the service valves and a small amount of a special oil have to be added to the system. Again, replacement of the receiver dryer/accumulator is recommended if the system has been opened to the atmosphere.

4. Another alternative is to wait for governmental approval of other refrigerants now coming to market. Manufacturers claim they're the same as FR-12, but full testing has not been completed.

5. You could, of course, just roll down your windows. You can't get much more environmentally friendly than that.

The major cost of any repair on the air-conditioning system will be the replacement of a failed component, such as the compressor or condenser. Replacement refrigerants cost only sightly more than what you paid for R-12 a couple of years ago. The only extra costs are the service valves (a few bucks) and the PAG oil. A fu-

---

In the old days you could recharge an air conditioner yourself, but those days are gone for good.

---

ture concern will be to see if service facilities charge to remove and recycle Freon (if you choose to stay with the old stuff). However, if you decide to convert to an alternative refrigerant, you may incur a hazardous-material handling charge for the storage of the old R-12.

It is strictly prohibited in the U.S. to mix the different refrigerants, and highly discouraged in Canada. In the U.S. the fine is $25,000 per incident or vehicle. This means that if a repair shop contaminates a 30-pound cylinder with different types of refrigerants and then charges ten vehicles with the mix, the fine will be $250,000. And that's not chump change.

Tracking down AC odor

Many cars develop a strong musty/moldy odor that wafts from the vents when the air conditioner is turned on. It's usually caused by mold spores nesting and reproducing, along with colonies of thriving bacteria, in the moist environment of the evaporator case. To get rid of the odor, you have to get rid of these microscopic critters. Find a repair shop that will use a spore-killing disinfectant. Unfortunately, mold spores tend to return, just like mildew in an enclosed shower stall. So schedule two treatments a couple of weeks apart—that should help for several years. Spraying a household disinfectant such as Lysol into the vents will help for only a short while. Other causes of odor include:

✔ The tube that carries drainage away from the evaporator can clog or get kinked. Have a technician straighten it out or unclog it.

✔ Debris can accumulate in the evaporator case. Clean it (p.70).

✔ A slight Freon leak in the evaporator case allows AC oil, which leaks out with the Freon, to collect dirt. The dirt holds moisture, and that makes it a breeding ground for mold.

✔ Parking on an incline sometimes prevents the water from draining away from the evaporator case.

✔ The evaporator case may be coated with too much corrosion protection. This will give an offensive odor that lingers for several minutes after the AC has been turned on. Install a new case to eliminate the odor.

Some moisture-related odors can be eliminated with an after-run blower relay. It lets the blower motor run for a few minutes after the car is shut off, evaporating accumulated water. A mechanic can add one.

Air-conditioning systems

Quick fix for heater icks

If water has accumulated in the air-conditioning system's evaporator case and is causing a musty odor, there's a quick fix that just might save you from having to undertake more extensive repairs.

Try this. Turn the heater on full-blast for a few minutes; then shut the car off. Now spray water from a garden hose over the air intake vents for a few minutes (they're the ones at the base of the windshield *outside* the car, not the ones inside!). This just might loosen up and flush any muck out of the heater/evaporator case and wash it away. If this doesn't work the first time, try it again.

The car pool

If the floor inside your car puddles with water, even when the sun is shining, there's a good chance that the drain on the air conditioning evaporator case is plugged. If so, moisture that condenses on the evaporator will fill the core and leak onto your feet.

Get the car to someone who specializes in an air-conditioner repair. The first order of business will be to see if the drainage system has been restricted by a kinked tube or a blocked line.

Also, the system sometimes includes a rubber check valve that must be looked at with trained eyes: it may be stuck in the closed position or have some tiny defect. The specialist should also apply sealer around the evaporator case where it sits against the cowl because this, too, is a prime area for water to leak into the car. Of course, if you'd just wear galoshes like your mother told you to, your feet wouldn't get wet in the first place.

 **Bob says . . .**

Don't do it unless you gotta

It's not necessary to convert an AC system to the new refrigerants just for the sake of change. This is not preventive maintenance; it's something that shouldn't be fixed if it isn't broken. That's because once you change from R-12 refrigerant to an alternative refrigerant, you can't change back. After the replacement service valves are screwed on, they'll destroy the existing fittings if they have to be removed.

Heating systems

Heating system checkup

Modern cars are built with many systems to provide comfort, convenience, and safety. One of the most important is the heating system. Its main job is to keep you warm, but it's also a very important safety device, clearing the windows of ice, snow, and fog. The heater core is an important part of the engine's cooling system, too. As the blower motor moves air across the core, heat from hot **coolant** is transferred into the car. The coolant is then recirculated back into the cooling system. The heater core can clog with rust and other deposits, just like a radiator. Some cars have mechanical or vacuum-controlled devices that will stop the coolant from entering the heater core on hot days; that makes the AC more efficient. Heater cores are difficult and very expensive to replace. To extend the life of your heater, back-flush the heater core when the rest of the cooling system is flushed.

If it seems to take too long for your car's interior to get warm, make sure there's enough coolant in the radiator and the recovery bottle; then make these four simple tests to be sure the heater is doing its job:

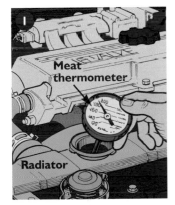

1. Warm up the engine with the radiator cap removed. (*Never* remove the radiator cap from a hot engine!) Stick a kitchen cooking thermometer into the coolant. It should be at least 180° F, and the upper radiator hose should be hot to the touch (be careful of the fan!).

If it isn't, you probably have a faulty **thermostat.**

2. Stick a kitchen thermometer in one of the interior heater vents. With the engine warmed up, the heater set on *Heat,* and the selector on *Vent,* the thermometer should read 100° F or more. If so, all is well.

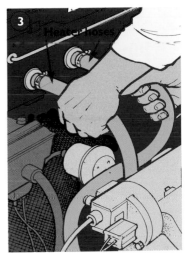

3. With the heater turned on, touch both heater hoses (they're under the hood.) If they're not hot, have a mechanic look for heater core or water control valve problems.

4. Operate each selector setting (*Vent, Defrost, Floor,* etc.) inside the car. If air isn't flowing to the correct outlet, or if the airflow changes speed or location as the car accelerates, have a mechanic look for vacuum control or linkage problems.

Chapter 6

Movin'...Engine and Drivetrain

Here's a secret. It's taught on the very first day of Mechanics College, after the students have sworn a solemn vow of silence, promising never to reveal it to the general, non-mechanicky public: "For an engine to run, it has to have three things: air, fuel, and spark."

Really, this is one of the biggest secrets to mastering auto repair. No engine will run if it's missing one of those three components, or if it's not getting one of them just when it needs it. A problem in any one of those areas means that you're not going anyplace, no matter how many times you turn the key or yell all those persuasive words you're so fond of.

Because most no-go (or not-going-very-well) automotive problems have their root in one or more of these three areas, you'll want to spend some quality time with this chapter. It provides plenty of insight, some how-to for quick checks and simple fixes, and some good advice about ways to prevent some really big mechanical problems.

Engine troubleshooting and tune-up

Tune-ups past and present

The tune-up, as many of us have come to know it, is a thing of the past, at least for the newer cars. It used to be that a car had to have a tune-up every 10,000 miles. This meant replacing the spark plugs, points, and condenser and adjusting the dwell, carburetor, and timing. Now computers linked to the engine make the adjustments as we drive. In fact, you may never again have to do a traditional tune-up.

Engines are now built to exacting tolerances; they burn fuel so efficiently that there's less carbon fouling and the **cylinder heads** run cooler, which prevents pre-ignition (pinging) and premature electrode wear on the plugs. Cars now get better mileage and pollute less. How's that possible?

Sophisticated electronic engine controls squeeze every drop out of every gallon of gas. In 1980 the first computer-controlled engines were introduced. The first onboard diagnostics (OBD I) sampled information sent from sensors on the engine. The **electronic control unit** (ECU) made adjustments to the engine through various control devices. Although OBD I was great, it was slow and not so reliable. Now there's OBD II, which can monitor all of the sensors, all of the time, and resolve potential problems while you drive.

The computer will turn on the "Check Engine Soon" light if it detects a condition that affects emissions. OBD II can even learn your driving habits and make minor adjustments to the fuel system to improve drivability.

But you still can't skip preventive engine maintenance. You still have to change the engine oil and filter; replace the air and fuel filters, **PCV valve**, crankcase filter, and charcoal canister filter; and visually inspect the spark plug wires, **EGR valve**, fuel cap, and fuel lines. Oh well.

In the know
Keep it clean

Excess carbon may cause a carbureted car to become awfully hard to start when the engine is warm. Yet when the engine is cool, it'll start right up. You had the car tuned, but now your mechanic says that you face an expensive engine overhaul. Hold on there, pardner: he may be jumping to conclusions. An accumulation of carbon on valves and valve seats can cause a loss of engine compression when a warmed-up engine is cranked, and that's what might be making it hard to start.

Luckily, treatment is relatively easy. It involves using an upper cylinder solvent, such as Gumout or GM Combustion Chamber Cleaner. Decarbonizing solvents can be added to the gas tank to help rid the engine of carbon. Try these products first to see if there's an improvement.

Warm up the engine to duplicate your hard-start situation. Turn the engine off, remove the air cleaner, and slowly pour solvent into the engine through the **carburetor** while someone else cranks the engine. The solvent will quickly dissolve enough carbon to allow the engine to start if carbon is, indeed, causing the trouble. *Slowly* pour in the rest of the solvent, without stalling the engine, and drive the car about 10 miles, revving the engine for brief spurts every 3 miles or so. If starting remains difficult, repeat the procedure, but this time draw the cleaner in through a hose connected to a **vacuum port**. If there's no improvement after two treatments, however, maybe your mechanic was right: sounds like you're in for some serious engine repairs.

Electronic ignition fixes

All vehicles built since the early 1980's have some kind of onboard computer and electronic ignition. If your car begins to run poorly, uses more gas than it does normally, or starts with difficulty, here are three simple checks you can make:

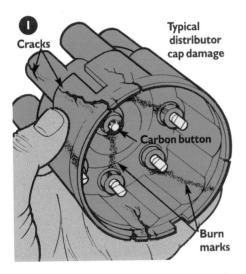

❶

Cracks

Typical distributor cap damage

Carbon button

Burn marks

1. Check the distributor cap. Remove it (usually by loosening a couple of screws) and look inside for cracks, wear, a powdery black trail (a sign of burning), or other damage. Check the carbon button in the top center of the cap as well. If in doubt, replace it. If you find a white crystallized substance in the cap (it's ozone), don't try to clean it—replace the cap.

2. Check the rotor next. It's inside the distributor body under the distributor cap. Again, look for signs of burning, wear, cracks, or other damage. Replace the rotor if it looks bad. Always replace the distributor cap and the rotor as a set; if one's bad, replace both.

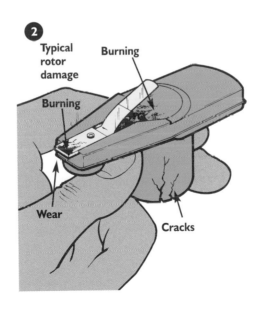

❷

Typical rotor damage

Burning

Burning

Wear

Cracks

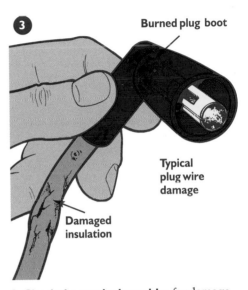

❸

Burned plug boot

Typical plug wire damage

Damaged insulation

3. Check the spark plug cables for damage, wear, or poor connections. Look for signs of cracking, burning, melting, or other damage. Also check for burning inside the plug boot. Plug wires carry high voltages, so don't pierce the insulation for any reason, with any kind of testing probe. If you find one bad plug wire, replace the whole set.

Engine troubleshooting and tuneup

Replacing spark plug wires

Spark plug

Modern spark plug wires are extremely durable—you would be, too, if you had to conduct 60,000 volts while trapped in the harsh environment beneath the hood. But if your vehicle has logged more than 50,000 miles, it may be time for new plug wires. When they start to fail, your engine starts harder, runs rough, misfires, uses more gas, and generates more pollutants. Whatever the mileage, if the wires are charred, cracked, oil-soaked, cut, or abraded, replace them.

1. Make sure your favorite auto parts store has replacement wire sets and a distributor cap in stock to fit your vehicle. Don't buy cheap plug wires. Get ones as good as or better than the originals. Most late-model vehicles use 8mm wires, and exact replacement sets with molded wires, boots, and snap-on terminals simplify things. Avoid the wire sets where you have to cut everything to size yourself. Typically, a matched replacement wire set costs about $7 per **cylinder**. More expensive high-performance versions are available, but they don't offer any major advantage in everyday use.

2. Label each old wire and its terminal on the old distributor cap with pieces of masking tape. This precaution will prevent hours of headaches figuring out which new wire goes where.

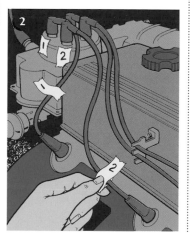

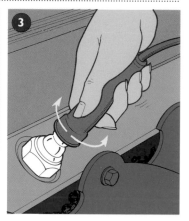

3. Gently twist and pull each spark plug boot—the rubber part that goes over the spark plug—until it comes free (above). Or use an inexpensive spark plug wire puller, available at auto parts stores. Never pull on the wire itself. Replace just one plug wire at a time, connecting it to the plug (now is a good time to replace the plugs as well) and to the new distributor cap. Be sure to route the new plug wires exactly the way the old ones were, including through the holders that keep the plug wires separated.

Platinum vs. regular plugs

Most dealers these days recommend that when it comes time to replace spark plugs, you replace conventional plugs with expensive platinum-tipped versions. Platinum plugs cost more, but dealers may tell you that they'll provide "more power" than conventional spark plugs; that seems to be the main selling point, anyway.

Car manufacturers are outfitting more and more of their new models with platinum-tipped spark plugs. And more and more service facilities are touting them as replacements when plugs have to be changed. But you'll often hear erroneous information like "more power." What you really want from any spark plug is the "hottest" spark it can generate, using the lowest amount of voltage. So let's get at the truth.

You can use either platinum-tipped or conventional spark plugs. You won't damage an engine by replacing platinum-tipped spark plugs with conventional spark plugs. You won't get

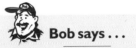

Bob says . . .
Wait for cool plugs

Always let the engine cool down before replacing spark plugs, especially on engines that have aluminum heads. The unlike metals expand and contract at different rates. Removed when hot, the spark plugs can rip the threads right out of the head, and that's not a very pretty sight.

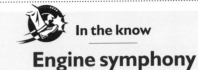

In the know
Engine symphony

Platinum is one of the best conductors known—at least when it comes to electrical current. During cold-weather cranking, extra current is drawn from the battery by the starter, lowering the voltage to the ignition system. One feature of platinum plugs is their ability to fire hotter at lower voltages: By burning all of the fuel in the cylinders, they can reduce cold-weather emissions.

any greater power, either, by replacing conventional spark plugs with platinum-tipped spark plugs. Your engine won't suffer a loss of performance until the spark plugs, be they platinum or conventional, wear out. So what will you get for the extra money you'll spend on the high-priced plugs? A longer period of time before they have to be replaced. Unless the plugs are damaged by some ignition system or engine malfunction, platinum-tipped plugs should be replaced, depending on the engine, up to every 100,000 miles, conventional plugs every 30,000 miles.

Whatever type of plugs you decide to install, make sure they're the right ones. They should have the same heat range and have the same reach (the distance between the end of the threads and the scaling surface) as the plugs being replaced. Be sure also that the air gap (the distance between the center electrode and the curved electrode) is set to the manufacturer's specifications.

Engine troubleshooting and tune-up

Emission tune-up

Vehicles built in the last few years are designed to go 100,000 miles between engine tune-ups. Sounds great, but now your focus should be on the various filters that need attention much sooner—every 15,000 miles or so.

I **Fuel filter.** Nowadays, most fuel filters are separate canisters, often closer to the fuel tank than to the engine. Usually you need to relieve the fuel tank pressure first. There may be a valve for this, but you can always do it by removing the fuel pump fuse (see your owner's manual), starting the engine, and letting it run until it dies. Clean off the filter's connections with a rag and some degreaser to keep dirt from getting into the fuel lines. Then loosen the connections, remove the old filter, and install the new one with the arrow facing *away* from the fuel tank. Start the engine and check for leaks.

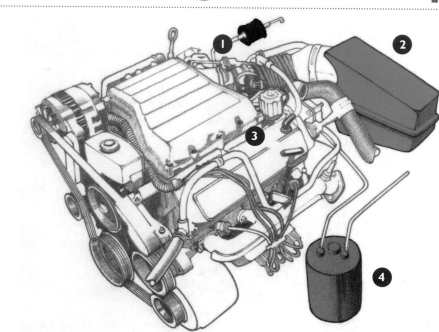

2 **Air filter and breather element.** Remove the cover and any fresh-air ducts. Clean the air-cleaner compartment of debris before removing the retaining clip on the breather. Install the new parts, and seal tightly so dirt can't bypass the filter.

3 **PCV valve.** It's usually in a rocker cover or the engine block. Carefully remove the valve from its grommet by twisting and pulling until it's free from the hose. Replace the valve with the exact brand and part number.

4 **Canister filter.** This filter stores fuel vapors when the engine isn't running (when it is, the trapped vapors are returned to the fuel tank and eventually burned as fuel). The canister is about the size of a coffee can, usually made of black plastic, and typically located across from the battery. Remove the screws that hold it in place (usually the hoses attached to the canister don't have to be removed), and carefully turn it upside down. Remove the filter and install a new one. In some cases you may have to cut the new filter to fit.

Replacing PCV valves and filters

The positive crankcase ventilation (PCV) valve and its filter must be replaced annually (or every 15,000 miles) if you want your engine to run properly. It costs only a few dollars, and replacing it takes just a few minutes. You'll usually find the **PCV valve** mounted in a rubber grommet on the valve cover (connected by a thick rubber hose to the air filter housing as in the drawing below), or built into the oil filler cap. You can replace it in 4 steps:

Remove air filter housing lid and air filter

Old PCV filter and retainer

1. Remove the locknut that holds the **air filter** housing and the air filter element. Now's a good time to check the air filter as well; replace it if it looks dirty.

Remove dirty PCV filter

2. Twist the PCV valve free from the rubber grommet in the valve cover. Be careful not to tear the rubber grommet or force it inside the cover. Once it's free, check the hose connector to the PCV valve for cracks or cuts, and replace it if necessary.

Here's a simple fix that has a big payoff.

3. Lift out the old, oily PCV filter from its retainer and replace it with the new one. If you have a version where the filter and retainer are joined, you'll have to disconnect the hose from the PCV valve and replace the retainer/filter as a unit. Usually the retainer is held in place by a spring clip on the outside of the air filter housing. Then reinstall the air filter and the housing cover.

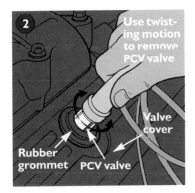

Use twisting motion to remove PCV valve

Valve cover

Rubber grommet   PCV valve

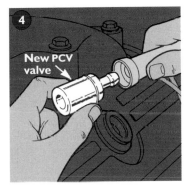

New PCV valve

4. Attach the new PCV valve to the hose, and then twist it into the grommet on the valve cover.

PCV filter inside

PCV valve   Air filter housing

Engine troubleshooting and tune-up

Charcoal canisters

The charcoal canister—an important part of your car's emission control system and installed in most cars built after 1974—traps and holds fuel vapors when the engine isn't running so they don't pollute the air. When the engine *is* running, these stored vapors are drawn into the cylinders, where they are burned off.

After 60,000 miles or so, the activated charcoal can lose effectiveness. You'll notice a gasoline odor under the hood when the canister begins to fail. A failed canister can lead to an overrich fuel condition at low speeds or when a cold engine is idling, either of which will cause poor performance. In newer cars this will usually cause the "Check Engine Soon" or "Service Engine Soon" light to turn on. Another reason to regularly replace the canister is the charcoal itself. After being subjected to years of vibration, it can break down into tiny particles and work its way into the fuel tank, eventually clogging the tank screen and fuel filter. Wise car owners won't neglect this part of the emission system.

You always hate to see big stuff go wrong on a car, but sometimes it's the small stuff that has the biggest effect on a car's performance.

Oxygen sensors

The oxygen sensor, or, as they're often referred to by mechanics, the "O_2 sensor," is one of several components in a typical computer-controlled engine management system. It's located in the engine's exhaust stream and keeps track of the fuel/air mixture. What data it gleans is sent to the electronic control unit (ECU).

The ECU then instructs the fuel system to make any necessary adjustments of the air-to-fuel mixture to achieve an ideal ratio of 14.7 parts air to 1 part gasoline (14.7:1).

There's no fix for a bad O_2 sensor. Because of its importance in performance, replacement every 50,000 miles is recommended. Actually, your engine will run with either a failed or a carbon-coated O_2 sensor. It'll run rich (and not as well) in this "limp-home" mode, but the engine won't suffer damage.

Most mechanics won't replace a sensor unless the malfunction indicator light is on. But unfortunately, the sensor can read "slow," which means it's keeping the fuel mixture either too rich or too lean, but not long enough to turn on the light. The clue is a sulfurous (rotten egg) odor. Here are some likely causes of sensor failure:

✔ The sensor tip can get clogged by carbon.

✔ Residue from silicone-based engine RTV (room temperature vulcanizing) sealers can crystallize on the sensor's louver end.

✔ Leaded gasoline is a no-no.

Also, if a head gasket fails or the engine constantly overheats, the porcelain inside the sensor can crack, making the sensor read backward; even the best technicians have a hard time finding this problem.

Replacing an oxygen sensor

Replacing the O_2 sensor on most cars is easy. The payoff is that once you do, your car will get better gas mileage, it will have more power, and the rough idling will (with any luck) disappear. As a bonus, you'll be doing something good for the environment because you will have reduced the car's emissions.

O_2 sensors produce an electrical signal that's triggered by a heat-activated chemical reaction. Usually one wire relays the signal to the car's ECU, though many newer cars have two- or three-wire sensors. The multiwire sensors are preheated, allowing the car's computer to take control of fuel management sooner instead of waiting for the engine to heat up. All vehicles with OBD2 emission systems have two O_2 sensors, one on either side of the catalytic converter. This allows the computer to monitor the converter's performance constantly.

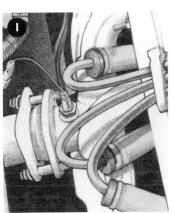

1. Detach the electrical connector. You may need a special wrench or socket (available at any auto parts store) to reach it. Make sure the engine is cool; then unscrew the O_2 sensor. You might have to struggle in order to bust it loose, but be persistent. If you're really having a hard time, try squirting a few drops of a corrosion-loosening lubricant on the threads—maybe that will loosen the critter.

2. Clean the exhaust system threads with an old toothbrush, a bottle brush, or a small wire brush.

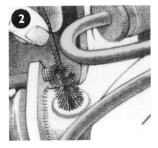

3. Dab antiseize compound on the threads, but don't touch the sensor tip or get any compound on the louvered end. Thread the new sensor into place until it's finger-tight; then torque it to 30 foot-pounds with a torque wrench (approximately one-eighth to one-quarter turn after the gasket makes contact); *Do not over tighten.* Reconnect the wiring harness, and you're done.

Engine troubleshooting and tune-up

White exhaust smoke

A few seconds of white smoke coming out of the exhaust pipe on the first start-up of the day is absolutely OK—it's just normal condensation burning off as steam, and it should go away as the engine warms up. Don't let your mechanic talk you into an unnecessary repair. If the smoke doesn't seem normal, though, have someone look at the car. But don't let anyone make repairs until specific problems have been identified. Here are some of the possibilities:

Vaporized antifreeze. This would be a lot of white smoke, heaviest on start-up but present whenever the engine is running. Thready, lingering smoke and a bittersweet smell signal that coolant is getting into the cylinders, possibly from a leaky head gasket. This is a serious problem; take care of it right away.

Thick white smoke would indicate an internally leaking transmission modulator. Transmission fluid is leaking into the vacuum pipe leading to the engine and is being burned in the engine on start-up.

Bluish white smoke would point to oil leaking past the valve guide seals and into the combustion chamber. This calls for the installation of new valve seals. An engine burning oil produces blue or blue-black exhaust that smells oily. If this is the symptom, you are probably adding oil more often than normal, the spark plugs are getting fouled, and the engine is idling rough.

Black smoke. This, along with a rotten egg smell, usually indicates an air/fuel mixture that is too rich. Related sypmtoms include poor engine performance, poor fuel economy, and spark plugs that seem to foul quickly.

Checking/replacing vacuum hoses

A ge takes its toll on rubber. Split, cracked, or loose vacuum hose connections can lead to improper idling, hesitation, and stalls. Vacuum hoses also supply systems like the heater, air conditioner, and power brakes. Replacing them is simple and can work wonders.

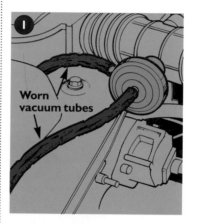

1. Check for cracked, split, or missing hoses. The emission information label (on or near the radiator cover) shows the hose routing. Hoses should be soft and flexible. Wiggle the hose connections; vacuum connections must be tight and leak-free. Replace any hoses that look bad or fit poorly. New hoses cost only pennies a foot. Take the old one with you to ensure a proper match.

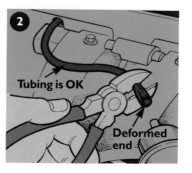

2. Pull each connection apart and inspect the tube's end. If the hose is hard to remove, split it with a utility knife or you risk breaking the part it's attached to—and that's expensive! If the tubing is mostly OK but the ends hold a flared shape or show signs of wear, cut about half an inch off .

Engine dies on turns

The reason an engine stalls when the car is rounding a turn is because the carburetor float isn't adjusted properly: it's too low. The problem that results is that there isn't enough fuel in the carburetor and the car literally runs out of gas when the small amount of the gasoline in the float bowl sloshes away from the fuel intake. After the car levels out, gas flows back into the intake and the engine starts up again.

Any halfway competent service technician would quickly identify this problem. The carb's float, needle, and seat (a small valve that closes when the gasoline reaches its proper level inside the carburetor) should be inspected and perhaps replaced, and then set to the service manual specifications. The inside of the carburetor should be checked for dirt and rust; replace the fuel filter while the carburetor is apart. The old fuel filter should be cut open and checked for signs of water contamination or abnormal amounts of sediment. This is a task that a competent mechanic can do with his or her eyes shut. The whole job should take no more than an hour or so, and it won't be costly even if a new float is needed.

Bob says . . .

Eureka! (or is it Hoover?)

Whenever the car has a drivability problem, no matter if it happens when the car is hot, cold, or in between, I always check for leaking or collapsed vacuum hoses. Many engine thermal- and emission-control devices are vacuum controlled. If they don't have enough vacuum, they simply won't work properly.

Cold-weather starting problems

The cause of a cold-engine, cold-weather starting problem on a carbureted engine is usually a faulty automatic choke or malfunctioning thermostatic air cleaner system. Here's how to handle the problem.

✔First be sure you're "setting" the choke first, by depressing (not pumping) the accelerator once before turning the ignition. Pressing on the gas pedal causes a bimetal spring inside the choke to slam the choke plate closed.

✔Parts of the choke system that may be impeding prompt starting are the choke plate and the choke linkage. If they're dirty, they'll bind and won't let the choke plate close. An overlooked part of the choke system is the vacuum break. As the engine begins to crank, engine vacuum pulls on the diaphragm of the break, which in turn pulls open the choke plate. The amount the plate opens is critical and must be set

exactly. The final choke service is to install a new bimetal spring inside the choke housing, if necessary. Have your dealer handle cleaning and adjustment of the choke.

✔A long-shot possibility on some four-barrel carbs is that the two galley plugs in the float bowl sometimes leak. All the fuel drains out of the float bowl, and the car must be cranked long enough to refill the bowl.

✔The reasons for a failed thermostatic air cleaner are legion. It could be a defective heat sensor, a disconnected or cracked heat sensor vacuum hose, a vacuum motor that isn't working, a disconnected or cracked hose between the sensor and the vacuum motor, a sticking damper valve inside the air cleaner snorkel, or a tear in the duct that runs from the snorkel to the exhaust manifold.

Engine troubleshooting and tune-up

Wet-weather starting problems

If your engine misses when it's damp outside, or quits and leaves you stranded whenever it rains, you can usually count on finding a problem in the secondary ignition system (spark plugs, wires, and plug covers; distributor cap; and coil). Here's what you should look for:

✔ The problem might be the absence of a shield over the distributor to protect parts from splash, which can cause the ignition to cut out. Install this part.

✔ A good way to pinpoint the trouble spot is to fill a spray bottle with water and then, with the engine running, spray water on wires, connections, and ignition components one at a time. You'll want to look for sparks arcing to ground, shaking, stalling, or a change in engine RPM. If the engine passes inspection of its ignition components, including the spray test, remove the engine air inlet tube between the power

module (it's located behind the battery) and the air filter box. Spray water into the power module—if the engine stalls, you'll know that the power module should be replaced.

✔ If the "wet test" didn't identify the problem component, have

every electrical connector in the engine compartment pulled apart to make sure the pins are straight and not corroded. The best tool to clean connectors and computer edge boards is the eraser on a No. 2 pencil.

✔ Have the onboard diagnostic system checked to determine if any fault codes are stored in its memory. This is always a good place to look. A fault code will tip off the mechanic to a defective electronic control.

The best tool for cleaning connectors and computer boards is the eraser on a No. 2 pencil.

✔ Have your mechanic adjust the idle speed control motor properly. Also, the throttle position sensor must have the correct resistance value and be the right one for your engine.

✔ Finally, have the fuel injectors cleaned to remove any contamination that might be present.

Knock bad

Engine noises—ping, knock, rattle, or any other assorted racket—can come from as many different places as there are moving parts beneath the hood. Here are some knock-knocks that are, unfortunately, quite common:

1 **A loose, dry, or overtightened V-belt** will cause a dull thud. Drive belt tension should be 95 pounds; the belt should have about 1 inch of play between the pulleys.

2 **Fuel injectors generate pressure pulses** in the fuel system. These pulses cause a fuel surge that leads to a hydraulic hammering noise in the fuel lines but doesn't signal impending failure. This metallic knock or rattle is clearly audible from inside the car. Strangely enough, you can't hear it when standing in front of the car, and you can barely hear it with the hood raised. Check with your dealer to see if there's a fix.

3 **A water pump bearing** produces a soft rhythmic knock at the front of the engine when it begins to fail. This should be looked into right away.

4 **A snapping or sharp rapping,** especially on start-up and acceleration, is most likely due to a cracked flex plate (flywheel) or loose torque converter bolts. A split engine pulley can produce the same type of noise.

Probably the most annoying noise is an engine ping. Engine ping (also called spark knock, detonation, and preignition) is caused by the premature ignition of gasoline in one or more cylinders by a source other than the spark plugs. It sounds like chains being dragged over a metal pipe. The "pinging" noise comes from the cylinder head, which vibrates as a result of the premature ignition. Some engines are equipped with a "knock sensor" that detects ping and adjusts the spark timing to reduce its effect. This is done so quickly that you can hardly hear the noise. Have the MAP (manifold absolute pressure) and EST (electronic spark timing) sensors, and if equipped, the knock sensor, tested to see if they're all working properly.

If the ping is barely audible when the engine is being accelerated and diminishes when you back off on the gas pedal, worry not: it's normal.

Knock worst

The most serious types of knocks, and typically the most expensive to fix, are ones that are deep within the engine. An engine shouldn't knock when the vehicle is rolling along at low speed, light-load conditions. A rhythmical thumping or thudding signals a problem that should be corrected before more extensive damage is done. Before reaching for your Sherlock Holmes getup, though, make sure the engine oil level is correct. If it is, you'll have to dig deeper to find the knock.

1 **First, warm up the engine.** Turn on the air conditioner, and set the temperature control at full *Cold* and the fan on *Low*. This may rule out the belt as the knock source. Put an automatic transmission in *Drive* or a manual transmission in first gear, and drive up a long, slight incline at 5 MPH or less. If you hear a heavy knock, the problem is lack of oil at the engine's No. 1 main journal bearing. Get thee to a mechanic before the engine is permanently damaged.

2 **A clicking, ticking, or tapping noise** indicates a valve, lifter, or rocker arm tap (either that, or your last mechanic is still in there working). Using an oil additive may rid the engine of this noise.

3 **Piston slap** is caused by excess clearance between the pistons and the cylinder walls. It causes a soft slapping noise, almost like a ping when the engine is cold. It's OK as long as it goes away once the engine is warm.

Engine troubleshooting and tune-up

The short and the long of it

Driving a car 1 or 2 miles to work 5 days a week constitutes what the manufacturers consider a "severe usage" situation. This isn't far enough for the engine to get hot enough to burn off the moisture that forms internally. This is especially bad news in cold-weather climates because the moisture causes oil to thicken and stick to engine parts, reducing lubrication and drastically increasing wear. Taking a longer route, or a long drive on the highway once a week, could be helpful. General Motors once issued a dealer service bulletin on this topic. Summed up, they advised that in cold weather, driving for at least 20 minutes is necessary to dissolve deposits, unburned gasoline, and moisture accumulated in the oil.

Water ends up in the engine as a by-product of combustion. For every gallon of fuel that is burned, 1 gallon of water is produced. About 90% of the H_2O is burned off as exhaust steam. The other 10% gets past the piston rings and into the crankcase. Moisture not burned off will coagulate into a thick tan-colored milky substance nicknamed "pancake batter." You'll see this stuff on the dipstick when you're checking the oil. It's oil mixed with water, *not* coolant. Also, using gasohol (p.54) produces more moisture than regular fuel.

Car manufacturers advise customers who typically drive only short distances to change the oil and the oil filter every 3,000 miles or 3 months, whichever interval occurs first. Assuming you drive at 50 MPH, you'd have to travel for almost 20 minutes for enough heat to develop to do the engine any good. A trip like this once a week isn't too tough to build into your schedule, is it? Short trips, by the way, are defined by the manufacturers as any trip of less than 10 miles when the air temperature is below freezing. A major culprit in all of this is the thermostat. Check to make sure it's operating properly (p.64). If the thermostat is out of calibration, the engine may never reach operating temperature no matter how far you drive.

If you have a new car, you may want to be even more conservative than the manufacturers. At the minimum, religiously change the oil and filter every 3 months.

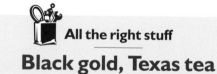 **All the right stuff**

Black gold, Texas tea

Sometimes engine noises are a characteristic of its design. Listen to other cars with the same engine to make sure you have a problem. The best, cheapest way to keep an engine in good shape, however, is to make sure the oil is changed at regular intervals. Use the correct weight and grade of engine oil. Too heavy an oil won't lubricate the bearings. Too light an oil will cause the engine to hammer for a few seconds on a cold start-up, causing modest damage that will eventually lead to big problems.

Belts

Stopping belt squeaks

Does your car make an annoying "Chirp, chirp, chirp" noise? No, you don't have a nest of birds under the hood, but you do have an engine drive belt that needs attention. The chirping may be because the belt is cracked, frayed, glazed (has a slippery, shiny look), or oil-soaked. If so, replace it, being sure to adjust the tension of the new belt properly. It's not too hard to do.

1. If the belt looks fine, (if you can't see any cracks, rough edges, or any other signs of wear), try the simplest fix first. If

Aerosol belt dressing

your car features the basic V-belt (the cross-section of the belt is shaped like a solid "V"), turn the engine off. Then give the belt a

Looking for chirps? Forget the trees—check the engine first.

shot of aerosol belt dressing. This product is available, usually for less than $10, at an auto parts store. On cars with the wider serpentine belts found on many late-model vehicles, use an aerosol silicone lubricant instead. But whatever the type of belt, make sure you don't lubricate it *too* much. If the belt or its pulleys get saturated, the belt could quite literally fly right off and damage other engine parts. So go easy on the stuff.

2. Still chirps? Check the belt tension (p.88) with the engine turned off. No belt should bend more than ½ inch when you push on the middle of the longest open stretch with your thumb. If there's too much give, adjust the belt tension until you reach that ½-inch-give level. Check the edges of the pulleys on the flat side (*not* the grooved side) of a serpentine belt; if worn, they may let the belt slide off the back of the pulley to rub against a bracket or some other part.

Belt tensioner

Worn serpentine drive belt

Rag dampened with aerosol brake cleaner

AEROSOL BRAKE CLEANER

3. Chirping not gone yet? OK, it's time to get tough. Remove the belt by loosening the tension adjuster. Dampen a clean rag with an aerosol brake cleaner (always wear rubber gloves for this) and thoroughly wipe the belt. Now do the same with the various pulleys and idlers where the belt goes. Scrape off any rubber residue that won't wipe off. Finally, lubricate any springs you see that obviously have to do with a belt tensioner, and reinstall the belt.

Belts

Belt tightening

That step-on-the-cat's-tail screech you hear as your car's engine starts means you should check the drive belts (but look for the cat just in case). Ignore these belts and you're guaranteed to have problems. But you can check them easily yourself and replace them if they're starting to wear out; here's how:

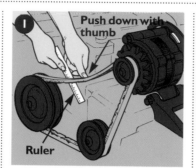

1. With the engine dead cold, push down firmly with your thumb at the center of the longest span of unsupported belt. It should move about ½ inch. Any less and it's too tight; any more and it needs tightening. You may want to have a ruler on hand to double-check your findings.

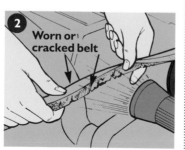

2. Visually inspect the belt — a flashlight or trouble light helps here. Twist it so you can look on both sides of the belt for frayed or cracked edges, splits or cuts, glazing (shiny areas), or patches of oil. If any of these conditions is present, replace the belt immediately, if not sooner.

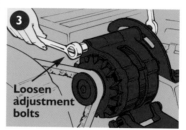

3. Adjust the tension by first identifying the pivot and adjustment bolts. What needs to be loosened is usually obvious or will be shown in the owner's manual. With a wrench, loosen the adjustment bolts so that the belt-driven device moves freely. Then retighten the bolts slightly.

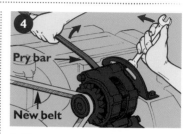

4. Place a pry bar where it can apply some leverage against the belt-driven device, but not where it might damage any engine components. Hold firm tension on the pry bar with one hand while tightening the adjustment bolt with the other. Once it's retightened, check the belt tension again and fully tighten all bolts. If you've installed a new belt, recheck the tension after 1 hour of operation. On vehicles with a single serpentine belt, proper tension is provided by a spring-loaded pulley. A slot in the pulley's bracket lets you apply tension to the belt before tightening the bracket mounting bolts.

Questions about timing belts

A timing belt is a rather important part of any engine, and if it snaps while you're on the road, the car will roll to a stop and won't go anywhere, except by tow truck, until the belt is replaced. "A nuisance," you say? It could be a catastrophe. Depending on the configuration of the engine, a timing belt that breaks could cause serious engine damage, and the subject of whether and when to replace an old timing belt is always a hot topic of discussion. To understand why, you have to know the difference between engines classified as "interference" and "non-interference."

On interference engines there's no clearance between the piston and the valves. When a belt quits on this type of engine, the valves and pistons smash into each other, destroying the engine. Non-interference (or free-floating valve) engines are designed so that if the belt snaps, the pistons and valves *won't*

smack into each other. On a non-interference engine it's only a few hundred dollars for repairs; on an interference design, costs can add up to *thousands* of dollars. It's worth the few hundred bucks or so to have the belt replaced at the recommended interval, if only to avoid the hassle of a broken belt and a dead engine during rush hour or late at night.

As a general rule, no matter what kind of engine is involved,

Replace this belt *before* it breaks—or replace your engine.

you'll have to replace the timing belt or chain at some point. Your owner's manual carries a specific warning about the timing belts, so make sure you take heed. Here are some guidelines:

1. If your engine has a cam that's belt-driven and the manufacturer

lists specific recommended replacement intervals (usually in the 60,000- to 90,000-mile range, or 50,000 miles on engines with overhead camshafts and four valves per cylinder), have it replaced as specified. Or maybe 5,000 to 10,000 miles earlier, depending on how cautious you want to be. This applies even if the engine is a non-interference type. Remember that if the engine quits, so do the power steering, the power brakes, and other nifty conveniences.

2. For engines with timing chains, there may be no specified replacement mileage. But most

mechanics will advise you to replace the timing chain if the engine is at or past the magic 100,000-mile mark. At about the 75,000-mile mark, you should start listening to the engine. A light knocking sound coming from the front of the engine, especially if it remains at the same intensity at any engine speed, indicates that the chain or gears may be worn and in need of replacement. Timing chains do break, causing engine damage or at least inconvenience.

3. If the owner's manual doesn't say, talk to two or three different dealerships or independent mechanics about what needs doing and when. Or contact the manufacturer's zone office listed in your owner's manual.

You can, of course, ignore all these recommendations. Lots of drivers do. But come on: Doesn't the do-it-now maintenance approach make more sense than the stranded-by-the-highway-in-a-snowstorm-at-night approach?

Belts

A guide to timing belts

Many cars have interference engines; many do not. The following is a *partial* list of vehicles that do have them. Many of the vehicles manufactured during the 1970's and '80's have timing belts (the others have timing chains or gears). See your owner's manual for the recommended change intervals for the timing belt. If the manual fails to specify it, change the belt every 60,000 miles. While we believe this list is accurate, there may be other interference engines not shown, particularly on cars of recent vintage. So again, refer to your owner's manual, your dealer, or the vehicle manufacturer for the last word.

Vehicle	Engine size (L=Liters)
Acura	All
Audi	1.6L Diesel, 2.0L Diesel, 2.8L
BMW	2.5L, 2.7L
Chevrolet	1.5L, 1.8L Diesel
Dodge	1.4L, 1.5L, 2.6L (1987–90)
Dodge truck	2.3L Diesel
Eagle	1.5L, 1.6L, 2.0L
Fiat	All
Ford	1.6L, 2.0L Diesel, 2.2L
Ford truck	2.3L Diesel
Geo	1.5L, 1.6L (U.S.); All (Canada)
GMC truck	2.2L Diesel
Honda	All

Vehicle	Engine size (L=Liters)
Hyundai	All
Infiniti	All
Isuzu	1.5L, 2.0L Turbo, 2.3L (U.S.); All (Canada)
Isuzu truck	2.2L Diesel, 2.3L, 2.6L
Lancia	1.8L
Mazda	2.0 Diesel, 2.2L (U.S.); All (Canada)
Mazda truck	2.2L, 3.0L
Mercury	1.6L (1981–85), 2.0L Diesel
Mitsubishi	1.5L, 1.6L Turbo, 2.0L DOHC
Mitsubishi truck	2.3L Diesel
Nissan	1.5L, 1.5L Turbo, 1.6L, 1.8L DOHC, 2.0L, 3.0L
Nissan truck	3.0L
Plymouth	1.4L, 1.5L, 1.6L (1987–90), 2.0L DOHC
Plymouth truck	2.3L Diesel
Pontiac	1.0L (1989–93), 1.5L, 1.8L Diesel
Porsche	All
Sterling	All
Suzuki	1.3L SOHO (U.S.); All (Canada)
Toyota	2.2L Diesel, 2.4L Diesel (U.S.); All (Canada)
Volkswagon	1.5L, 1.5L Diesel, 1.6L Diesel (U.S.); All (Canada)
Volkswagon truck	All (except Vanagon)
Volvo	2.1L Turbo, 2.3L, 2.3L Turbo
Yugo	All

Drivetrain

When to replace transmission fluid

Automatic transmissions are expensive to repair because of their complexity. Just like an engine, they require periodic maintenance. Changing the filter and fluid every 12 months or 15,000 miles is crucial for extended life. In addition to lubricating the transmission, automatic transmission fluid helps to transfer energy from the engine and keeps the transmission cool. This is one case where you should turn to your dealer to do the work, rather than leave it to a quickie oil-change place.

Here are a few tips on how to tell when it's time to change, regardless of mileage. Drip a few drops of the transmission fluid onto a clean white piece of paper. Here's what these spots will tell you:

1. Clear, pinkish red, or green: The color varies by type used, but when it looks like this it's probably still OK.

2. Milky white, pinkish: A "milk shake" condition. It's probably a leak in the transmission cooler (the cooler is inside the radiator) that's letting coolant mix with the transmission fluid. Have this fixed right away.

3. Dark reddish brown: If it has a burnt aroma and looks burnt, it's overdue for a change. The fluid has lost its ability to lubricate.

4. Metal particles visible: Uh-oh! This could be bad news, a sign of high wear and possible damage. Some metal debris is normal, so first get the fluid and filter (inside the transmission pan) changed right away. Drive a few thousand miles, and then have another fluid/filter change. If there's still a lot of metal debris in the fluid, take it to your dealer for an evaluation and possible repair.

Quick tip

Save some for the next fill

Never overfill the transmission. Too much transmission fluid will cause air bubbles to form in a process called "fluid aeration." It makes sense: fluid lubricates, air doesn't.

Driveshafts: care and feeding

Driveshafts (for rear-wheel-drive cars) and drive axles (front-wheel-drive cars) transfer the power of the engine and transmission to the drive wheels. Except for a few vehicles that have universal joints (U-joints) that must be greased periodically, there's no service or maintenance required to keep a driveshaft healthy. It must be inspected during normal service for damaged constant velocity (CV) joint boots (it's way cheaper to replace a boot than a defective joint), worn universal joints, dents, or road debris getting wrapped around the shaft. You also want to check for leaks where the shaft enters the transmission.

The driveshaft must be kept clear of undercoating. Because a driveshaft spins up to four times faster than the tires, any debris stuck to it will throw the shaft out of balance, causing vibration.

To check for bad U-joints, place the car on a slight incline. With your foot on the brake, move the transmission shift lever back and forth between *Reverse* and *Drive*. If you hear a loud sharp clank or snapping sound, that indicates that the U-joints are worn. To check for a faulty CV joint, listen carefully for a crunching or grinding noise on slow, sharp turns. These joints can't be repaired, so replace one if faulty.

Drivetrain

Clutches don't last forever

All manual transmissions need a **clutch**. Located between the engine and the **transmission**, the clutch disc and pressure plate transfer power from the engine's flywheel to the transmission and make it easy for you to shift the gears. Like brake linings, there is no set mileage for which a clutch should be expected to last. Good driving habits will increase its life. If you're experienced in using a clutch and feel you should get more mileage before replacing it, have your service technicians examine all clutch parts. Here are some things you should have them check:

✔**A defective engine flywheel.** The flywheel should be checked for contamination, grooves, warpage, heat damage, and hard spots. Flywheels, like brake rotors, can be refaced at a local machine shop.

✔**A defective clutch release** (throwout) bearing or fork. Replacement is a pro's job.

✔ **Loose bolts.** Bolts that join the pressure plate and the flywheel can work loose. If they're easily accessible, you can tighten them; otherwise it's for a pro.

✔**Weak or failed pressure plate springs.** Your mechanic will have to replace them.

✔**Worn input shaft splines.** The front bearing retainer or the input shaft pilot bushing may also be worn. If this is what your mechanic finds, get ready for a really big job—turn it over to a manual-transmission specialist.

Don't be a klutz with your clutch

A clutch most often fails due to misuse. If your car has a manual **transmission**, here's how to keep the clutch healthy:

1 Be sure the amount of clutch pedal travel (free play) is adjusted to manufacturer specifications. Have it checked when you have the engine oil changed. On cars that have a hydraulic clutch, however (many do), no adjustment is possible—talk to your mechanic.

2 Never rest your foot on the clutch pedal. This is called "riding the clutch" and it causes clutch friction material to wear away prematurely.

3 Don't rest your hand on the gear-shift knob, either. This bad habit stresses the transmission synchronizers and causes unnecessary wear. Really!

4 Engage and disengage the clutch quickly and smoothly Clutch slippage creates heat, heat hastens wear, wear eventually hits you in the wallet.

5 As you shift gears, pause for a fraction of a second in *Neutral* before engaging the next gear, giving the transmission synchronizers a chance to get into sync with each other.

6 When stopped on an uphill grade, don't slip the clutch to keep the vehicle from rolling back. Use the brakes instead.

7 Don't rev the engine as you shift. This may sound snazzy but it's a clutch killer.

8 Don't lug the engine in a gear too high for the speed you're traveling. It's your constitutional right to shift as much as you have to in order to keep the RPMs up.

9 When accelerating from a stop, don't just dump the clutch in an attempt to increase acceleration—always release it smoothly and gradually.

In the know

Avoiding clutch problems

One way to squeeze more mileage out of every tank of gas is to drive a car with a manual **transmission** instead of an automatic transmission. The manual versions are more fuel efficient, so more and more cars are being built with manual transmissions. But manual transmissions have their own set of headaches. The biggest one is **clutch** chatter, not to be confused with a slipping clutch.

Clutch chatter is a jerking, shaking, or shuddering that occurs, sometimes violently, on acceleration or clutch engagement. Usually it's due to a worn **clutch pressure plate**, **clutch disc**, or release bearing, but there are three other causes to consider:

✔ Oil on the clutch. Engine oil from the rear main seal, transmission fluid, or hydraulic oil from the clutch slave cylinder or line, which causes a burned or glazed clutch disc.

✔ A loose or broken engine mount, damaged or misadjusted transmission linkage, or loose bell housing bolts.

✔ A worn transmission input shaft or splines.

During every oil change, check the clutch slave-cylinder hydraulic oil, and adjust and lubricate the linkage.

Living with a manual transmission

Forward gears in a manual **transmission** are synchronized. As you shift, their rotational speed is matched to the speed of mating gears to keep them from clashing as they engage. Cadillac was the first to introduce this feature, back in 1930 on the V-16 model (yep, 16 cylinders!).

Reverse gear, however, is not synchronized, so you sometimes have to fuss a little to shift into it. One trick is to first shift into a forward gear and roll forward a bit before shifting into reverse. If you're parked too close to another vehicle, try pushing the **clutch** in and then pausing for a few seconds before you shift. Why? After you push on the clutch pedal, the clutch disc will keep spinning for as much as 9 seconds before it stops. If the clutch disk is spinning, so are all the gears in the transmission; if you just let them slow down a bit, they'll engage more easily.

Living with an automatic

Computer-controlled shifting in a modern automatic **transmission** makes driving dreamy, but this mechanical marvel needs some care.

Check the fluid level each month. Put the car on a level surface, set the parking brake, place the shifter in *Park*, and let the engine warm up. With the engine running, pull out the transmission dip-stick; *be very careful to avoid moving engine parts when you do this.* Top off the transmission fluid as indicated.

If your car has an overdrive gear, use it to improve fuel economy even if most of the driving you do is around town.

Stop completely to shift from *Reverse* to *Park*. Never shift into gear while racing the engine.

Drivetrain

Gears: down but not dirty

What do you call the last car in the drivetrain? (Hint: "Caboose" is wrong). If you said "gears," you're right. The proper term for these gears, however, is **differential**. This assembly is what finally applies the engine's power to the axle, and it's the axle that leads to the wheels. In a rear-wheel drive car, the differential is that bulbous case that sits between the rear wheels, connected to the transmission by way of the drive shaft. On a front-wheel drive car, the differential and the transmission are located within a single housing; together they're called the **transaxle**. Whatever kind of car you have, though, take proper care of the differential. All internal moving parts are lubricated by oil that's splashed around during normal movement of the gears. Maintaining the proper oil level, and changing it when it gets dirty, will let you enjoy years of problem-free driving.

Gear oil should be checked during every scheduled service, or every 7,500 miles, and changed about every 2 years or 30,000 miles. If you take your vehicle off-road, tow a trailer, or do most of your driving in the city, change the oil sooner. Many front-wheel drive cars have a dipstick and filler tube under the hood, making it easy to check and add fluid if necessary. On other cars look for one or two plugs on the differential, or (on front-wheel drive cars) two plugs on the transaxle. In either case, you'll have to shinny under the car to reach them. Clean off the plug closest to the top of the car. Remove it (careful—the oil might be hot) and stick a bent pipe cleaner into the hole. The oil should be no more than ½ inch below the fill hole. Fill to the correct level using the proper grade of lubricant, and never overfill the unit. When you're done filling, make sure the fill tube or plug is properly seated so oil won't leak out, and so water and road dirt can't get in.

Cars today use many different types and grades of gear oil. On rear-wheel drive cars, it may be single- or multi-weight gear oil (usually 75-90 weight). On front-wheel drive cars, it can be gear oil, engine oil, or even automatic transmission fluid. Check your owner's manual or call the dealer to determine exactly what type of lubricant is best for your gears.

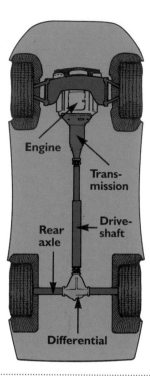

Car with rear-wheel drive

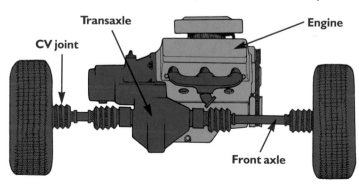

Car with front-wheel drive (view from rear of car)

All about posi-traction

Posi-Trak is the General Motors name for a limited-slip differential. Other manufacturers may call it Posi-Trak, Positraction, Traction-Lok, Anti-Spin, Twin-Grip or something else. Whatever the name, though, it's purpose is to provide traction when one rear wheel of a vehicle is spinning and the other has traction. It's available only for some models of rear-wheel-drive vehicles, especially pickups.

Special gears allow the rear wheels to rotate at different speeds, but divide the engine power equally. While turning a corner, the outside wheel travels farther and rotates faster than the inside wheel. That's fine when there's plenty of traction, but not so good when, for example, one wheel is on ice and the other is on dry pavement. In this situation, the ice-bound wheel is spinning at twice the normal speed, while

the wheel with traction doesn't move at all, increasing stress on the differential gears and bearings. The vehicle goes nowhere. Spinning the wheels wildly generates tremendous heat, quickly breaking down the gear oil and damaging the differential. If the wheels do grab while spinning at these speeds, the impact can rip the teeth right off the gears or snap an axle.

A limited-slip differential is usually identified by a metal tag attached to the differential assembly. Vehicles with a limited-slip differential require a special lubricant or additive for proper clutch operation. So when you take the vehicle in for an oil change, tell them that the vehicle has a limited-slip differential—in case the differential needs some lubricant. The type of lubricant that should be used is spelled out in your owner's manual. The rear should be drained and refilled at the first 7,500 miles, and then every 15,000 miles thereafter, and sooner if you tow a trailer. Fluid not providing proper lubrication (either the wrong type or worn-out gear oil) will cause the clutches to slip, producing a grabbing or chattering noise. This does not mean there's a problem, but you'll want to have the rear serviced as soon as possible.

In the know...

Traction trick

A limited-slip differential contains a clutch that allows power to move from the wheel that's slipping to the wheel that has traction. That's usually enough to get the vehicle moving. But in some cases there isn't enough torque (turning force) in the spinning wheel to trigger the clutches. If that's the situation, try this trick: Engage the parking brake a few clicks. This will momentarily keep both wheels from spinning, and that will let the clutches energize. Then step on the gas pedal *slowly,* and as soon as you start to move, release the parking break. You'll be on your way.

Chapter 7

Tires, Wheels, Brakes, and Suspension

Going and stopping is what a car is all about, but there's more to it than "Go" and "Whoa!" You can turn only as safely as your tires will let you, and you won't glide over potholes if the suspension is shot. Your trips won't be much fun, either (or very frequent), if you can't stop at the end of them. Yet these three critical systems—tires, brakes, and suspension—are probably the ones most ignored by the typical car or truck owner. Look around the next time you're stopped at a light. Pick any three vehicles; one is almost certain to be driving with worn-out or damaged brakes, and it could be gobbling brake shoes like candy. It sure doesn't have to be that way.

Tires, especially, are critical to your driving safety and enjoyment. And all you really have to do is to regularly check and adjust the tire pressure, rotate them occasionally, and replace them before they're worn (and unsafe). Pretty simple when you think about it . . .

Tires

Tire college

Read any good tires lately? Embossed on the tire's sidewall you'll find coded descriptions of the tire's tread, temperature performance, and traction rating.

Traction and temperature ratings go from A (highest) to C (lowest). Don't buy C-rated tires; their wet-weather traction is lousy. A tire with a tread wear rating of 300 will last twice as long as one rated at 150, all else being equal. To establish the ratings, manufacturers test tires on a 7,200-mile course under specified conditions.

Bias or radial? To buy a tire you also have to know about tire construction. There are three types of tires: radial, bias ply, and belted bias ply. The plies (or layers) consist of belts and cords that stabilize and strengthen the tire in different ways. These plies can be made of various materials. Because radials roll easily, they improve fuel economy. They also

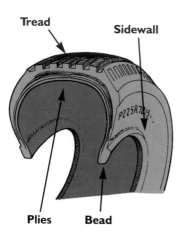

Tread | Sidewall

P225R7815

Plies | Bead

wear longer, corner better, and stop faster—no wonder they're standard issue on all new cars.

Caring for tires. Inspect your tires every time you fill up. Look for abnormal wear, bubbles on the sidewalls, cuts, or embedded nails. When the tread has about $\frac{1}{16}$ inch of thickness remaining, tire-wear indicator bars appear as a solid strip of rubber across the face of the tread: time for new tires. Here are some buying tips:

✔New tires should always be installed in pairs.

✔All tires on a vehicle should be the same width, diameter, and design. Don't mix and match.

✔All four tires on a vehicle used to tow a trailer should have the same load rating.

✔Snow tires should be the same size and design as the other tires. If you install larger- or smaller-diameter tires, that could affect the speedometer's calibration.

The tire rotation two-step

Tire manufacturers recommend that you rotate radial tires using a cross-rotation pattern or a modified "X" pattern. Cross-rotating will even out wear and prolong tire life. The exact rotation plan depends on your vehicle, so check your owner's manual. If you have to replace the rear tires, move the current front tires to the rear and put the new tires on the front. After driving another 5,000 miles, rotate the tires using a modified "X" pattern.

To get the maximum mileage from your tires, it's best to rotate them every 5,000 miles, or sooner if you notice a wear problem. Have them balanced if you feel a vibration while driving at highway speeds.

If you aren't sure which rotation plan to follow or if you have a problem with your tires, write the Tire Industry Safety Council, P. O. Box 1801, Washington, DC 20013. In Canada, call the Transport Canada Road Safety Directorate (800-333-0371).

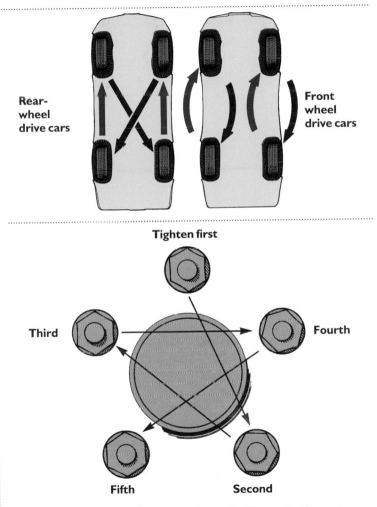

Rear-wheel drive cars

Front wheel drive cars

Tighten first

Third

Fourth

Fifth

Second

Tighten lug nuts in a "star" pattern. If the wheel has only 4 lug nuts, tighten them in opposing pairs.

Uneven wear on the rear tires

When tires are unevenly worn, the car feels unstable at highway speeds. This wear, called cupping, is fairly common on the rear tires of front-wheel-drive cars. That's largely due to the up-and-down motion of the rear suspension, but it could also be the result of underinflation, fast starts, and wheels that are out of balance.

There's no way to undo cupping damage, but if it's not too bad, try this. Swap the two rear tires (the left rear becomes the right rear, and vice versa). The tires will now rotate in the opposite direction, which might even out the cupping over time. This works only with the rear tires, however; swapping front tires could make the car hard to control.

Tires

Tire siping

In the 1920's, John Sipe worked in a meat-packing plant. Tired of slipping on wet floors, he discovered that cutting tiny slits in his rubber-sole shoes improved footing significantly. Recognizing that the same concept might work on automobile tires, he spent years developing a series of machines that cut very fine slits, or "sipes," across the tread surface. The technique is still popular, but is it worth the few bucks per tire that it costs?

Tests published in the U.S. by the Committee on Winter Driving Hazards of the National Safety Council report that passenger cars equipped with four siped tires showed improvements in traction and stopping distances, but ribbed highway tires and wide performance tires benefited the most. All-season mud and snow (M&S) tires don't benefit as much.

Most tire companies aren't keen on siping, however, and won't warranty any tire intentionally altered after manufacture. So buy good tires in the first place and forget about siping.

Before siping

After siping

Check the air in the spare

Perhaps the most neglected item on a car is the spare tire. It's usually tucked beneath a ton of junk in the trunk, so nobody ever checks its air pressure. Well, getting stranded on the side of the road late at night is not the time to find out the spare is flat. Keep a tire gauge in the car (it costs only a few bucks), and check the spare's air pressure every 6 months and before taking a long trip. Be sure the valve core isn't leaking after checking the pressure (see p. 102). Your owner's manual will give you the proper inflation pressure (usually 60 PSI for a "mini" spare), plus instructions on how to remove and install the spare.

Cold weather and tires

You may need this information only a few months out of the year, but it's important to keep some facts about cold weather and tire care in mind:

✔ Pressure should be checked when the weather turns colder in the fall and winter, because tire pressure decreases about 1 PSI (pounds per square inch) for each 10°F the temperature drops. A tire that's correctly inflated when it's 70°F will be underinflated by as much as 5 PSI at 20°F.

✔ Whatever the weather, tire pressure should be checked with the tires cold. The best time is first thing in the morning or after driving no more than a mile.

✔ Lower tire pressure does not improve traction in the snow—this is a popular misconception. When the car is loaded, underinflation can cause the tire bead to break away from the wheel.

Causes of uneven tire wear

Unless you've been driving on seriously underinflated tires (see right), rapid, uneven tire wear suggests that the car has been in an accident and the frame-alignment repairs weren't completely succcessful. Chances are the body shop will claim otherwise, so here's a simple do-it-yourself test to see if the repair was done correctly.

1 Inflate all the tires to their recommended pressure (use an accurate tire gauge); then pour a puddle of water on a dry concrete surface. Drive the car through the puddle onto the dry surface for about 100 feet.

2 Check the marks the tires left. You should see two straight, clearly defined tracks. Any fuzziness (if they look like a photograph that's out of focus) hints at a damaged undercarriage. Keep in mind that this is a crude test. But if it indicates a problem, the next step is to have the chassis checked on a frame rack at a body shop. A body shop using a laser measuring system can determine if the car is out of original specifications by measuring multiple points around the car simultaneously. First-rate body shops will have such a machine. That should give you all the evidence you need to confirm the problem and convince your insurance company that the frame alignment has to be redone.

It's difficult to straighten a vehicle that's been in an accident that damaged the undercarriage. So, you have three options, none of them very attractive:

1. Drive the car as it is, replacing tires when needed.

2. Have the repair made again. Maybe the second time around it'll be done right.

3. Get rid of the car.

**Excessive wear at center:
Over inflation**

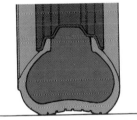

**Excessive wear at both edges:
Under inflation**

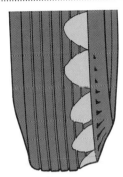

**Scallops: Tires not rotated or
suspension needs service**

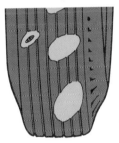

**Bald spots: Defective tire or
unbalanced wheel**

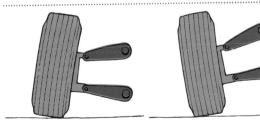

Excessive wear at one edge: Too much camber (angle between wheel and pavement

Tires

Water in tires

Take notice if water is expelled from the air hose along with the air when you fill your tires at the local service station. Water, and especially the dirt it often carries, is harmful and can damage the interior of a tire.

Moisture is a by-product of compressed air and can accumulate inside the compressor's tank and lines. Most air compressors at service stations have filters to trap this moisture, but it doesn't hurt to test the air hose anyway. Use the little nub on the body of a tire air pressure gauge, or something similar, to press the valve core of the air hose to let out some air. Be sure it's not pointed at your face! If water spritzes out, get your air someplace else.

If you'd rather do your tire checking and filling at home, get an accurate tire pressure gauge and an air compressor (small ones are $50 or less). This is easier and less of a hassle than going to a service station.

Leaky tire cure

Got a tire with a slow leak? Before you take it in for an expensive repair, check for a leaky valve core—that's often the source of slow leaks. A set of four new valves and caps, along with a valve repair tool, is inexpensive. Get them at an auto parts store.

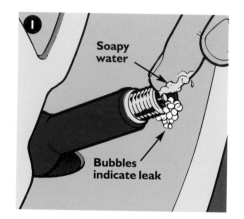

1. Remove the extensions or cap, and dribble soapy water on the valve. A leaking valve core will produce bubbles. If the valve is leaking, place a jack stand or the vehicle's jack (check the owner's manual for proper positioning) under the car for support; you needn't lift the car up. Let the air out; then unscrew the core using the valve repair tool. Be careful, though: the valve core can fly out and injure you!

2. Screw in a new core (but don't overtighten). As you fill the tire to its proper pressure, your car will lift off the jack stand. Retest the valve with soapy water; then replace the cap. Always keep the valve covered with a cap to seal out dirt.

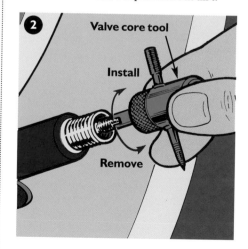

Wheels

Stopping wheel cover rattles

If the clickity-clickity-click sound your car makes as it rolls down the road isn't coming from something like a nail in the tire or a worn **constant velocity (CV) joint**, a wheel cover is the likely villain. To confirm this, pry off the wheel covers and go for a test drive. If the clicking has stopped, you now know the cause. Here's how to fix it.

1. Car maker emblems are sometimes separate pieces clipped or screwed to the wheel cover. If an emblem is loose, retightening it often stops the clicks.

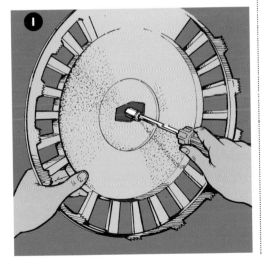

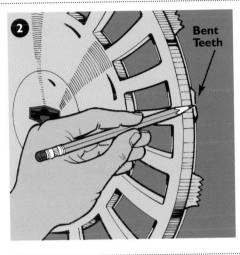

Bent Teeth

2. The sawtooth clips that hold a wheel cover to the wheel are a more likely source of noise. Sometimes the clips are riveted to the cover; sometimes they're part of the cover itself. Either way, if the teeth are bent or folded over, they won't bite into the wheel rim firmly enough. This lets the cover move around slightly as the wheel rotates, generating the clicking sound.

3. Riveted clips can be tightened by carefully hammering the rivet flatter. You'll need something behind the rivet (the edge of a vise, for example) to back it up while you hammer the front. With clips that are part of the wheel cover, carefully bend the teeth back into their proper shape with pliers—you may have to pry the clips open first. To reinstall the wheel cover, make sure it's fully seated against the wheel rim and that the tire valve is properly aligned with the wheel cover's hole. Use a rubber mallet to seat the cover firmly.

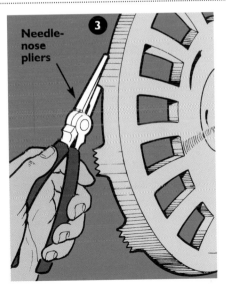

Needle-nose pliers

Wheels

Alloy wheel repair

Alloy wheels are pretty durable. After a while, though, an accumulation of chips and scuffs can leave them looking tired. Professional refinishing can cost hundreds of dollars, but you can often fix them up yourself.

1. Wash wheels with a special cleaner for alloy wheels. Alloy wheels may have an epoxy-like clearcoat (and sometimes an accent color) that gets chipped or scraped. You have to repair these chipped areas before the exposed alloy becomes stained or oxidized.

2. Clean and repolish the exposed alloy with 400-grit sandpaper or a Scotchbrite pad. Feather the edges back toward the undamaged finish; then wipe the area clean with rubbing alcohol.

3. Spray automotive clearcoat (or matching color enamel) into a cup, and repaint the damaged area. If the area is large, mask the surrounding surfaces and spray the wheel with several light coats. Whenever the wheels are balanced, use only plastic-coated wheel weights to eliminate oxidation where the weights are attached.

Keep alloys sparkling

Keeping your aluminum wheels looking great can be difficult. Oxidation and brake dust can really dull and darken their appearance over time. If you can't restore the shine with regular car-wash detergent, try one of the special polishes and cleaners made specifically for aluminum; they're available at auto parts stores. These products can be very caustic, however, so follow the directions on the product's label to the letter. Note that aluminum polish works only on alloy wheels that don't already have a protective clearcoat. Check with your dealer if you're not sure whether there's a coating on your wheels.

✔Clean dirty or dull wheels thoroughly with a spray cleaner designed for aluminum wheels. It works fast and eliminates elbow grease and scrubbing pads. But this is strong stuff, so don't get it on your car's finish (and be sure to read the label for any other cautions). Spray the cleaner carefully from the bottom of the wheel to the top, let it work for a minute, then hose it off thoroughly. (These cleaners are not for use on molding.)

✔After cleaning the wheels, polish them (and any molding) with aluminum polish. Several brands are available; experiment a bit to find the one that works best for you.

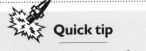

Lug wrench spinner

Here's how to remove automotive wheel lug nuts quickly and with less effort. Cut an 8-inch piece of 1½-inch-diameter PVC pipe and glue a cap to one end. Slide the pipe over the end of a lug wrench and you can spin the wrench easily. This useful little device can be stored right in the spare tire compartment.

End cap

1½"-dia. PVC pipe

Removing lug nuts with ease

Remember the last time you struggled to remove a lug nut from a flat tire? Or to remove a spark plug? Or to loosen just about anything where one type of metal surrounds another metal? Well, mechanics come across this kind of thing all the time and they have to struggle, too. It's not that everybody is getting weaker (well, probably not...); it's just that the metal bond has been getting stronger because of corrosion, heat, and chemical reactions (electrolysis) between unlike metals (such as between an aluminum wheel and its steel hub).

The solution is to apply antiseize lubricant on metal fasteners or components as you assemble them. This lubricant is great for spark plugs on engines with aluminum **cylinder heads**, **oxygen sensors**, wheel lug nuts, and any other part exposed to heat or corrosion.

Lug nuts are the worst, though. First clean the bare

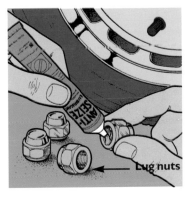

Lug nuts

threads with a wire brush before removing the lug nut; this keeps the nut from stripping. Once the nut is off, apply enough antiseize lubricant to coat the threads of the fastener. (*Never* use oil on lug-nut threads; the nuts could loosen and come off as you drive.) Antiseize lube is thick, sticky, silvery stuff that won't wash away, and it resists heat and corrosion. It comes in a can with a brush applicator, in a tube, or as an aerosol spray and the stuff can cost as little as a few dollars at an auto parts store. Use it whenever you're assembling metal components.

Brakes

Identifying brake problems

It has been estimated that more than a third of the vehicles on the highway have brake problems. Is yours one of them? Look for the telltale symptoms. If any are present, get your car to a professional. And get a high-quality brake job—good brakes can save your life. Brakes should be checked twice each year (more often if you're hard on them), even if none of the following symptoms are present.

✔ Rhythmical vibrations or pulsation that you can feel through the brake pedal (unless your vehicle has **antilock brakes**, where these are normal) could mean the **brake rotors** or **brake drums** are warped.

✔ If the brake warning light on your instrument panel stays lit after the engine starts, the brake system could have a serious hydraulic pressure problem. It might also stay lit if you're really low on brake fluid.

✔ Squealing sounds when the brakes aren't being used is the brake wear indicator: it's time for routine brake service.

✔ Brakes that pull the car to one side, grab suddenly, drag, or lock up prematurely are dangerous. Have a mechanic check for hydraulic fluid leaking onto the brakes, sticking disc brake calipers, collapsed brake hoses, or **wheel cylinder** problems.

✔ An occasional squeak or squeal from disc brakes when braking lightly is normal. Loud screeching, grinding, or shuddering isn't, and may mean **brake pad** or **brake shoe** problems.

✔ A squeaking or clicking noise from the rear of the car when releasing the brake pedal signals a lack of grease on the rear brake shoe backing plate. This can lead to overheating and lockup.

✔ Any change in the feel of your brake pedal may indicate trouble.

A pedal that is high or difficult to press down could mean a power brake problem. A constant hissing when the pedal is held down says "Danger: Vacuum leak in the power **brake booster**." A pedal that goes nearly to the floor might be caused by poorly adjusted brakes or a hydraulic failure. A spongy pedal is a sign of air trapped in the brake system.

✔ "Dog-tracking" occurs when both rear wheels seem to lock up at the same time when the car is cold. It usually occurs after the front pads have been replaced and is most likely a temporary condition that will correct itself after a few miles of driving.

Pedal pulsates

✔ A car that pulls to one side probably has a brake problem but might instead have a loose, worn, or weak suspension part or faulty alignment. Seek service.

Checking brake fluid

Your car's brake system depends on brake fluid for the hydraulic oomph that translates pedal pressure into stopping power. It doesn't take much of a mechanic to figure out that if the fluid is faulty, or if it just isn't there, the brakes won't do what they're supposed to do: stop your car. Whether your car is new or old, fast or funky, or even four-wheel-drive, take a minute now and then to check the brake fluid. It takes only a moment but could save you plenty of time, money, and aggravation:

The **master cylinder**, which is bolted to the power brake booster, is on the driver's side of the car, near the **firewall**. That's where you'll find the brake fluid reservoir. Every few months, remove the cover of the reservoir (if it's clear, just look through it) to determine the brake fluid level. Before you remove the cover, however, wipe it clean so no dirt falls into the fluid. If the fluid level is low (it should be no more than ½ inch below the top of the reservoir), then either the brake linings are worn or there's a leak somewhere in the system. Brake fluid does not evaporate.

Act promptly. If linings wear excessively, **brake rotors** or **brake drums** will be damaged. When that happens, what would have been an inexpensive repair becomes *very* expensive. If a fluid leak exists and isn't fixed, you'll notice a loss of braking performance at first, then a complete loss of braking power. Not good.

If fluid must be added, use only what the owner's manual recommends from a fresh, *sealed* container (brake fluid absorbs moisture and contaminates easily). Adding mineral-based oils or fluids (transmission or power steering fluid) to the brake system will cause the brake fluid to boil or will swell rubber components and ruin them.

Brake booster step-through

Most of the time, when a car isn't moving and the engine is running, you can push the brake pedal down until you feel and hear it hit something. No, this isn't a problem. It's called "booster step-through" and is normal in cars that have power brakes. Here's the story behind what's going on.

When you apply moderate pressure to power brakes, you move a push rod that causes vacuum power to move another push rod; the two push rods never touch under normal conditions. But by stepping down hard on the brake pedal, you'll move one push rod forward until it actually hits the other. This metal-to-metal contact is what you hear and feel. It doesn't do any damage and it won't affect braking.

Vacuum-assisted power brakes are essentially a normal hydraulic brake system fitted with a **brake booster** unit that generates energy by opposing engine vacuum and atmospheric pressure. This setup can develop up to 1,500 PSI of brake pressure. Here's a simple test to check the power brake booster. Push down hard on the brake pedal with the engine off. With your foot still on the pedal, start the car; the pedal should move down somewhat. If it doesn't move, or if it goes all the way to the floor, have your brakes checked by an expert right away.

If you don't take care of your brakes, you'll hear about it (and so will the car stopped right in front of you).

Brakes

Everything you wanted to know about brake squeaks and squeals but were afraid to ask

Squeals or squeaks that you hear every time you apply the brakes are annoying. You can have your dealer pull the wheels off and inspect the brakes if the sounds seem unusually loud. But if the dealer reports that nothing can be done to squelch the squeals, he's probably right.

A GM advisory memo to its dealer service departments puts brake squeal and squeak into perspective. Although these are comments from GM, they apply to brakes in all makes of cars. Here's what the advisory says: "The design criteria for brakes includes government requirements, service life, space limitations, noise level, heat transfer and cooling, stopping ability, pedal effort and feel, fade resistance and environmental effects. The choice of **brake pads** is ulti-

mately a balanced choice, but priority must be given to those criteria which affect braking performance under the Federal Motor Vehicle Safety Standards.

"The brake pads used on today's vehicles may cause an occasional and intermittent high-pitched squeak or squeal when brakes are applied with light or moderate pressure. If the brake system is functioning correctly and it is the judgment of the dealership's service department that the demonstrated condition is normal brake noise, the customer should be assured that this is an operating characteristic of disc brakes and no repair should be attempted." The advisory goes on to say that trying to eliminate normal brake noise will result in temporary improvements at best.

Various governments have restricted the use of asbestos for

brake components in new cars and aftermarket replacement parts. Squeak is the price we've had to pay for ridding the environment of asbestos, which had been used extensively as the primary material in the manufacture of disc brake pads and **brake shoes**. Asbestos was replaced by metallic linings, which were in

turn replaced by semi-metallic linings. Until recently, brakes manufactured with semi-metallic material had a tendency to squeak loudly, especially in damp weather, but recent designs have cured that. Semi-metallic pads now outlast asbestos pads by many, many thousands of miles, cutting down on the frequency of brake jobs.

Parking brakes: Use 'em or lose 'em

Parking brake, emergency brake, whatever you call it, they all work the same way. The hand or foot lever pulls a steel cable, which causes an actuator inside the rear brake assembly to press against the drums or discs. If your car has four-wheel disc brakes, always set the parking brake when you park the car; this activates a self-adjusting mechanism and maintains proper brake operation. Keep your foot off the brake pedal when you release the parking brake, though, or the self-adjusting mechanism won't work properly.

Whether you have disc or drum brakes, don't set the parking brake after driving in slush or snow unless necessary for safety. Ice may build up around the brake cable, causing the rear wheels to lock up when the temperature falls. If your car has rear drum brakes, the rear brake linings can freeze to the **brake drums** and make it impossible to get the car moving until they thaw. Have your parking brake checked as a regular part of your service routine. Among other things, a mechanic will look for damage or wear in the plastic-coated linkage cable.

Turn the drum lightly, if at all

Brakes on a new car will probably have plenty of lining left even after 30,000 miles. You can thank metallic-hardened brake linings for the good mileage—before they were in widespread use, it was common to need new brake linings every 15,000 or 20,000 miles. But you can also thank these linings for a minor problem. Newer cars, especially those equipped with semi-metallic rear brake linings, may develop symmetrical ridges on the brake drums. It's called "scoring," it's normal, and it doesn't affect brake effectiveness, but your mechanic will probably want to resurface, or "turn," the drums at some point anyway. Turning **brake drums** and **brake rotors** refers to using a brake lathe to remove ridges and other defects, and it makes the metal smooth enough to match new linings. Not long ago, turning drums and rotors was standard operating procedure when doing a brake job.

But beware: turning the drums on some cars can create big problems. Here's why

Many smaller cars come from the factory with rotors and drums that have barely enough surface to meet minimum refinishing specifications. If they're turned anyway, normal driving will soon wear them *below* the specs considered safe. If these brakes seem to be wearing normally, and they aren't vibrating, pulling, or grabbing when you stop, there's probably no reason to turn the drums or rotors.

Always go to a repair shop that has the latest in brake repair equipment. On front-wheel drive cars, particularly those with **antilock brakes**, the brake rotors should be dressed with a non-directional finish if the rotors and/or drums were turned. Insist on this extra step: it eliminates tiny grooves that actually reduce the amount of surface the brake linings can contact.

Suspension

Shocks & struts: The bump stops here

If every road were smooth, straight, and glass-flat, your car wouldn't need **shock absorbers** But real life comes with shocks because at the tightest spot in every uphill hairpin turn there's a pothole big enough to swim in. Shock absorbers (and their close cousins, **struts**) are what keep you from losing control of the car every time you hit a hole or a speed bump, but they're also crucial for keeping the car level when you slam on the brakes.

Your car might have either four shocks (typical of most rear-wheel-drive cars), two front struts and two rear shocks (semi-independent suspension), or four struts (front-wheel-drive with independent suspension). Once the shocks or struts wear out, the car will bounce noticeably as you drive. Weak springs can cause the same problem, but it's usually the shocks or struts that go first. Try this. Push down on your car's front or rear bumper as hard and as far as you can, then let go; the car should come to rest after one bounce. If it doesn't, *maybe* the shocks are bad (if they leak, they're definitely bad). To know for sure, they have to be removed and tested. Yep, that's a lot of work, and more often than not, shocks/struts are damaged during removal and can't be used again. That's why most folks rely on the bumper test even though it's not definitive.

You can buy many different types of shock absorbers. Most standard shocks rely on hydraulic oil to smooth out the ride. Newer gas-charged shocks use low-pressure hydrogen to keep the oil from foaming during vigorous up-and-down movement. Self-leveling shocks have a valve that maintains normal curb height when the car is loaded with gear or passengers. Adjustable shocks can be set for a hard or soft ride. But the most common *replacement* shock is the load-leveling or air shock. Compressed air can pump up the shocks as needed to stiffen the suspension when carrying extra weight; remove the extra air for normal driving.

Choose a shock based on the kinds of loads you usually carry and the way you drive. If your car is old and the shocks or struts have never been replaced, put new ones in. If that fails to improve the ride quality, you're probably due for new springs. Springs aren't cheap, though, so you'll have to decide if your car is worth the expense.

Shake, rattle, and roll

When the front of your car hops or bounces above 25 MPH or so, or the steering wheel vibrates, that's a sign of an unbalanced wheel assembly. There are other possibilities, of course (aren't there always?) Maybe it's a driveshaft out of balance, or a faulty engine mount, or even some **transmission** malady. It could be something in the suspension or the steering system. (Regarding the latter, a good wheel alignment specialist should be able to find such suspension problems as worn tie-rod ends, worn ball joints, a loose steering gear, or a damaged **CV joint**). Vibration might even be caused by the engine; if it's misfiring, maybe that's what you feel. But because about 75% of all vibration problems are related to the tires or wheels, you ought to start there.

Have the tires checked with a tire problem detector. This machine reveals the radial (up-and-down) runout and lateral (side-to-side) runout of tires and wheels. Lateral runout is usually the reason for a shimmy at low speeds. If the machine shows that radial runout is greater than .050 inch, the tire is unacceptable and should be replaced. Radial and lateral runout test results for wheels should be compared to manufacturer allowances that are spelled out in the service manual.

If the tires are OK, the wheel assembly (the tire, wheel, and the brake rotor or drum) should be balanced. One method is called static balancing. Tires and wheels are removed from the vehicle and mounted on an electronic balancing machine; then small weights are added to the wheel to bring it into balance. This often does the job, but not always. That's why it's usually a good idea to have the wheel assembly both statically and dynamically balanced.

Dynamic balancing requires a spin balancer. The car is raised and the spin balancer is shoved against the car to spin the wheel assembly up to highway speed. A strobe light is used to determine if even a slight

imbalance exists. Some vehicles are so sensitive that even a minor deviation from true balance will cause a vibration. Again, weights are used to bring the assembly into proper equilibrium.

If you are really, truly determined to find a vibration that no one can put a finger on, find a shop that has a Reed Tachometer (a dealer usually has one of these gizmos). This nifty device measures the frequency of vibrations and can pinpoint the source.

All of this work and diagnosis will be expensive. Only you can decide if the problem is bad enough to merit pouring money into a solution. If you've had the problem since the car was new and have been trying to solve it, you may be able to persuade the dealer to help out with the cost of additional investigation even if the vehicle is out of warranty.

Electrical Stuff

An engine may run on gasoline, but it won't even start without a reliable flow of electricity. Just think of all those happy electrons sprinting from the battery to the starter motor as their buddies head for the distributor and spark plugs. If they don't arrive when and where they're needed, you're in trouble because no electricity means no go.

Want to listen to cool tunes? You need juice for the radio and tape player. Just want to cool off? The fan that circulates the cool air is electrically powered. In fact, today's vehicles fairly bristle with all manner of electrical and electronic goodies, all of which depend on a steady flow of electricity. Read on for a rundown on how to keep everything humming the same tune.

Batteries

Choosing a battery

A car battery is the heart of your car's electrical system. It produces and stores electrical energy and stabilizes voltage in the vehicle's electrical system. Most batteries in today's cars are either low-maintenance or maintenance-free designs. Low-maintenance batteries have removable cell covers that let you add water if necessary. Introduced in 1972, maintenance-free batteries are totally sealed; water need never be added. That's due to a fundamental change in the design of the battery's innards: By changing the battery's plate configuration, "gassing" was eliminated. Gassing (the process of changing water in a battery into hydrogen and oxygen) creates heat, and it's the heat that caused the water to evaporate. Nothing, though, is absolutely maintenance-free, and these batteries still need occasional service.

Batteries are rated by three measures. *Reserve capacity* is the approximate time in minutes that a fully charged battery will operate a car, with minimum electrical load and the **alternator** not charging. *Ampere-hour rating* is a measure of how much current a battery can supply before it is seriously weakened. *Cold cranking amps* is the minimum amperage a fully charged battery needs to maintain at least 7.2 volts at 0°F for 30 seconds.

Always try to replace your old battery with one having a higher reserve capacity, ampere-hours, and cold cranking amps rating than the original—never smaller. The physical size of a battery is also very important. It must fit properly using the correct battery hold-down.

Before you replace a "faulty" battery, though, consider this. If you habitually leave the dome light on, or take a lot of short trips (that's hard on a battery), or let the battery slide around in its tray, maybe *you* are the problem.

Battery maintenance

All automotive batteries, even the maintenance-free types, ought to get a yearly once-over. The most important part of the maintenance involves the terminals. Corrosion in this area is bad news. Here's what to do:

If the battery isn't sealed, unscrew the cell covers and check the fluid level: it should cover the tops of the metal "plates" visible inside. If not, add distilled water

Corrosion on the terminals can stop you dead.

(it's cheapest at the supermarket). If the battery is a sealed type, maintenance is limited to Steps 2 and 3 on the facing page.

A battery maintenance tool kit: A few dollars spent at any auto parts store or department-store auto department will give you everything you need. And even though the tools are cheap, buy good ones because you'll be using them for years to come.

The shopping list:

✔Battery terminal puller (unless the battery has front- or side-mounted terminals). Loosen the terminal nuts; then use a puller instead of trying to pry the terminals off with a screwdriver, which could easily crack the battery case.

✔Wire battery brush, preferably the type with both internal and external bristles. The former fit over the terminal; the latter fit inside the cable clamp.

✔White grease, petroleum jelly, or other corrosion-fighting product to apply to the terminals.

✔Specific gravity tester (called a hydrometer). It's inexpensive and simple to use (it looks like a turkey baster). Buy one that comes with instructions.

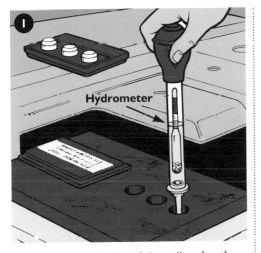

1. Check the condition of the cells using the hydrometer. Measure each cell and write down the reading. If the readings between any two cells differ by more than .05, replace the battery. If the readings indicate a low state of charge, you may be able to have the battery recharged, but maybe it's on its last legs. Check the water level; top it off if necessary.

2. Replace the cell cover and then clean the battery case with a mixture of baking soda and water, after plugging the cell cap vents with toothpicks. Flush the case with plenty of cool water (never use high pressure) when finished, and wipe dry. A dirty battery case will lessen the battery's charge because the grime provides a path for current to leak between the terminals, slowly discharging the battery.

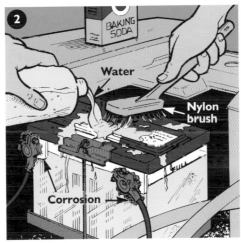

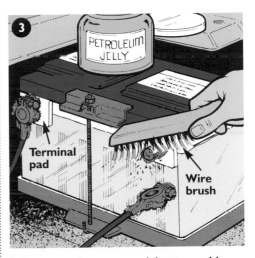

3. Loosen and remove each battery cable.
Clean the battery post and cable clamp/terminal with the battery brush, or use a wire brush or steel wool, removing any corrosion. On front- and side-terminal batteries, the electrical contact is the terminal pad, not the battery bolt. Apply a film of petroleum jelly to each post/terminal and then reattach the cables. Tighten the bolts carefully—don't King Kong them to the point where you crack the case or break the clamps.

Batteries

Build-it-yourself battery memory keeper

Whenever a battery is disconnected for repairs or replacement, all the various memory devices—the clock, your favorite radio stations, even some engine functions—will be lost. Annoying, eh?

The solution is to supply a bit of current to those instruments via a homemade unit that plugs into the cigarette lighter socket. You can buy one ready-made for less than $20, but you can make one for about half that in just a few minutes. Here's what you need, from either your spare parts drawer or an electronics store:

✔ 9-volt battery

✔ 9-volt battery connector

✔ lighter socket plug

✔ shrink tubing

✔ two 1-foot pieces of electrical wire, in two colors

✔ soldering iron (or soldering gun) and electrical solder

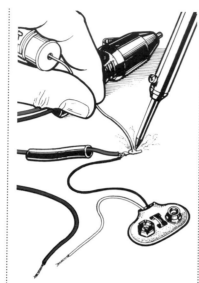

1. Solder the red wire from the battery connector (the positive terminal) to the wire from the positive side of the lighter socket plug. Do the same for the other wire. Have the shrink tubing in place on the wires before you begin soldering.

2. Heat each piece of tubing with a match or a heat gun to create a tight seal over each soldered connection. You could instead use vinyl electrical tape.

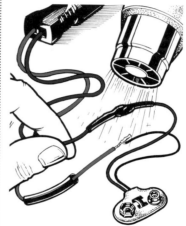

Too bad it won't make *your* memory any better . . .

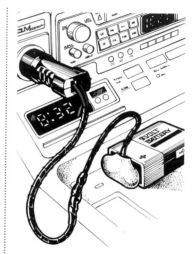

3. Before disconnecting the vehicle's battery, put a fresh 9-volt battery into your memory keeper. Plug it into the cigarette lighter socket, and it'll keep all of the electronic memories intact.

Caution: Don't use this for more than an hour at a time.

Battery ground cable problems

Electrical shorts and bad grounds can make a car do all kinds of goofy stuff. Like when you turn the key to start your car and nothing happens—no cranking, no warning lights, even the door chime is silent. Then you'll get a jump start and all is well for a few weeks. Your mechanic can't find anything wrong with the battery or the **alternator,** so he's given up. This kind of intermittent problem will make even the best mechanics cringe. But the cause in this case is usually one of two things: Either a short circuit is draining the battery or there's a faulty ground.

Checking for a short is easy. First, charge the battery. Then disconnect the negative cable. With every electrical component in the vehicle switched off and the doors shut, hold a 12-volt test light (inexpensive, and available at auto parts stores) tightly between the negative battery termi-nal and its post. If the test light glows, you've got a short circuit causing a drain on the battery. That's the simple part. But finding a short is like finding a needle in a haystack, so take the vehicle to a shop that specializes in electrical systems—track one down in the Yellow Pages.

If the test light doesn't glow, stop and think a minute. Does the problem strike most often during or just after rainy or humid spells? If so, corrosion on an electrical ground is the culprit.

Electricity is tricky, and tries to complete a circuit any way it can. This is called "finding the path of least resistance." But too much resistance in a circuit (caused, perhaps, by corrosion) causes heat buildup, and even fire if the heat becomes too great. That's not just expensive; it's dangerous.

What could cause this problem? Well, for a battery ground cable to get hot enough to burst into flame, the current flowing

through it must be hampered by resistance somewhere. Look for these possibilities:

1. The cable is undersized or is made of aluminum wire. Your dealership can make sure that the correct cables are installed.

2. The cable is kinked. Although a gradual bend is OK, the cable must not have any extreme bends. Make sure the protective cover has not rubbed through at any brackets, allowing the cable to contact the body.

3. There are four connections that become dirty and/or loose and should be checked: two for the negative cable on the battery and engine, and two for the body ground cable on the chassis and engine. Find those points and clean them thoroughly, like this:

✔ With the cable removed from the car, sand the spot on the engine to which the cable attaches until the spot is clean. If the spot is coated with paint, sand until you reach bare metal.

✔ Using sandpaper or a wire brush, clean the ends of the cable, the threads, and the end of the screw that attaches the cable to the engine, along with the screw that attaches the cable to the battery (if one is used).

✔ To ensure a good, tight connection, install an external-tooth lock washer, available at any hardware store, between the screw and the cable.

Batteries

Jump-starting a car the safe way

Way too many people get hurt every year trying to jump-start cars. But jumping a car using the battery of another car isn't difficult if properly done. If the weak battery has a built-in hydrometer "eye" that's clear or bright yellow, however, don't jump-start the battery; it's shot.

1. Maneuver the helper car near the car with the run-down battery. Don't let the two cars touch. Metal-to-metal contact creates a wayward ground, diverting current needed to boost a dead battery and start the engine.

 Caution: Remove all rings, necklaces, watches, and other jewelry. Engines have moving parts that can catch anything loose.

2. Turn off the ignition switch, lights, and accessories in both cars. Place both transmissions in *Park* or *Neutral* and engage the parking brakes. Don't smoke: Batteries produce gases that are flammable and explosive. Battery acid is very caustic. Wear eye protection and flush anything the acid contacts with plenty of water.

3. Connect a clamp of the red (positive) jumper cable to the positive terminal (marked + or POS) of the weak battery (**A**). You can twist the clamp *slightly* so it gets a better bite on the terminal, but don't get carried away. Attach the cable's other red clamp to the + or POS terminal of the helper car (**B**). Never let the jumper cable clamps touch the car body, each other, or the other battery terminal. Keep metal tools from touching the + or POS terminal. **Caution:** Don't connect cables to a frozen battery—it can explode!

4. Connect a clamp of the black (negative) jumper cable to the negative terminal (marked - or NEG) of the helper car's battery (**C**). Connect the other clamp to a clean metal part on the engine in the car with the weak battery (**D**). Get the clamp as far from the battery as possible; the alternator bracket or an engine bolt works nicely for this.

Caution: Don't attach the negative jumper cable to the - (NEG) terminal of the weak battery. If you do, sparks that may fly when the metal clamp touches the terminal could ignite hydrogen gas given off by the battery. Many people have been killed or injured by battery explosions.

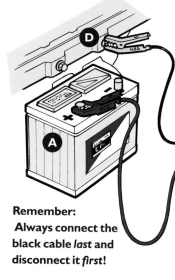

Remember:
 Always connect the black cable *last* and disconnect it *first*!

5. If possible, put a damp rag over the vent holes in both batteries to keep gases inside.

6. Start the engine of the helper car and rev the engine a little. Then try to start the other car. If it doesn't start, turn off the ignition of *both* engines and make sure the jumper cable clamps are attached securely. Try again. If the engine starts, wait to make sure it doesn't stall, then disconnect the jumper cables in this order: negative cable from the ground connection, then from the - (NEG) terminal of the helper car; positive cable from the + (POS) terminal of the helper car, then from the + (POS) terminal of the other car.

Buying booster cables

Every vehicle should have a set of jumper cables on board for those times when someone needs a jump start. But some cables are better than others. The heavier the wires in a cable, the more current it will deliver. The following guide will help you decide which cables are best for you.

	GAUGE	QUALITY
	10	Good
	8	Better
	6	Best
	4	Professional

Features:

✔ The best cables use either 4- or 6-gauge wire (the smaller the gauge number, the thicker the wire); 8-gauge cables may be OK in warmer climates.

✔ Cables should be at least 12 feet long; 16 feet is better.

✔ They should be tangle-proof and have a carrying case.

✔ Get clamps that will work with top, front, and side battery terminals.

✔ Clamps should be color-coded and clearly labeled.

Long jumper cables are safest because they allow hookups when the cars can't be nose to nose, as when the disabled car is alongside a freeway.

Quick tip

Space jump

The engines of many newer cars are packed in so tightly under the hood that there's no room around the battery to hook up a jumper cable. Look instead for jumper blocks; they're usually covered in red plastic and marked with a big + or (POS). That's where the positive cable should be connected. When in doubt, however, check your owner's manual.

Lights and blinkers

Bad headlight connections

Does your car go through sealed-beam headlights as if they were popcorn at the movies? Maybe it's because of a corroded or damaged headlight connector. Everything you need to fix it is at your auto parts store. Here's what to do:

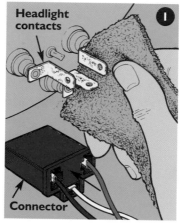

1. Inspect the back of the headlight bulb. Look at the contacts on the bulb and the connector it plugs into. If there's corrosion or dirt, clean it off with a plastic abrasive pad or emery cloth; then flush with an aerosol contact cleaner. To prevent future corrosion, apply some dielectric grease to all the contacts.

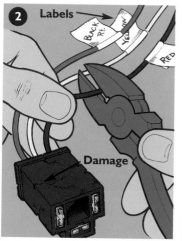

2. A damaged connector (frayed or missing wires, broken or corroded metal contacts, or cracked housing) is easy to replace. A new three-wire connector is inexpensive. Label the wires with masking tape so you know where they attach to the connector, then cut off the old connector. Strip about ½ inch of insulation from the wires of the new connector.

3. Slip the shrink tubing onto each pair of wires, then twist the wires together lengthwise. Solder the wires, and when they're cool, slip the shrink tubing over the joint. Use a heat gun or a match to shrink the tubing. Apply some dielectric grease to guard against new corrosion.

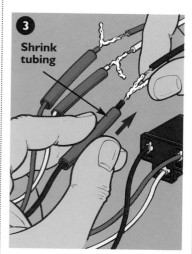

Even a small amount of corrosion can keep your headlights from getting all the juice they need. The fix may be easier than you think.

Replacing a broken sealed-beam headlight

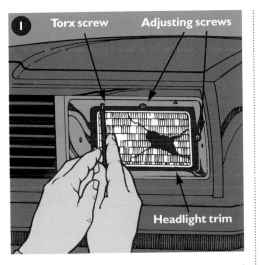

1 Torx screw   Adjusting screws

Headlight trim

1. Remove the screws that hold the trim panel surrounding the headlight. (Note: Some vehicles have headlights that are removed from the "inside" — from under the hood. Or the headlight may have a separate bulb, rather than being a sealed-beam unit. Check your owner's manual if there doesn't seem to be any way to remove the headlight.) These screws may be one of the specialized types, such as the star-shaped **Torx**. Sears and most hardware and auto parts stores sell multiple-bit screwdrivers to fit. Once you have the trim piece off, you'll see three or four more screws

surrounding the headlight. Two of these screws (the ones with springs around them) are for adjusting the headlight's aim. Leave them alone and remove the others.

2. Pull the headlight forward slightly to expose the electrical connector at its back. Unless there's obvious damage to the headlight, the problem may be a loose connection or corrosion on the contacts. Loosen and remove the connector, check for corrosion or dirt, then reattach it to the headlight and check the light again. If there's still no light and the connector seems fine, the headlight is probably a goner. Take it with you to the auto parts store and get a good-quality replacement. Buy a

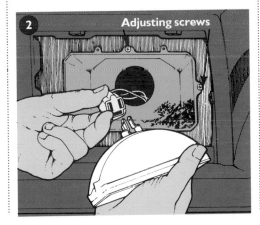

2 Adjusting screws

halogen type for a brighter light. If the headlights on your car are more than 2 years old, replace all of them.

3. Spray electrical contact cleaner into the electrical connector to flush out any corrosion. It's also a good idea to spray some WD-40

3 Adjusting screws

or other lightweight lubricant on the various mounting and adjustment screws to help ward off corrosion. Reattach the electrical connector to the headlight, being careful not to twist and push too hard because it's easy to break off the terminals. Then reinstall the headlight. As long as the trim's off, now is a good time to make sure the headlights are aimed where they'll do you the most good (see p. 123).

Lights and blinkers

Halogen lamp replacement

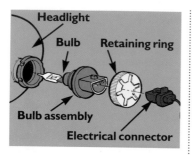

Headlight
Bulb   Retaining ring
Bulb assembly
Electrical connector

Halogen headlights have become common since the mid-80's. They're a bit more expensive—$12 to $16 each—but have a brighter, longer-lasting light that doesn't fade with age. If you have halogen-bulb headlights and one fails, don't look in front for the trim and retaining screws, as you've come to expect with the older sealed-beam headlights. Instead, open the hood and check the back of the light. You probably won't need any tools to replace the halogen bulb.

1. Unlock the retaining ring— usually a quarter turn to the left—and slide it back to expose the bulb assembly. Then simply wiggle the assembly straight back to remove it from the headlight. Don't touch the glass of the old bulb, just in case it's not the bulb that's at fault but something else. The natural oil on your hands will shorten the life of any halogen bulb.

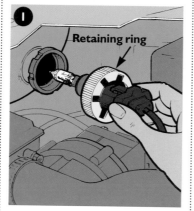

Retaining ring

2. Unplug the bulb assembly. Lift the plastic locking lug and unplug the old bulb assembly from the harness. Replace it with a new assembly, and slip it back into the bulb socket. Slip the retaining ring forward and relock it with a quarter turn to the right.

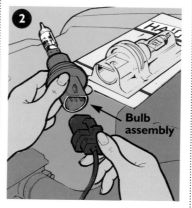

Bulb assembly

Watch it!—you can ruin a bulb just taking it out of the package.

3. So what happens if the headlight still doesn't work? There are several possibilities:

✔ In replacing the old bulb, you may have damaged the new one. Halogen bulbs are fragile and have to be treated properly. Touching the bulb's glass with your fingers can cause the bulb to quickly burn out.

✔ Assuming the new bulb is sound and the correct one for your car, the malfunction may be with the connector into which the bulb assembly plugs. If the high beam on the other side of the car is working, unplug the bulb assembly. Examine the contacts on the plug. If you see corrosion, rub it off with a pencil eraser. If this doesn't work, have your mechanic install a new connector.

✔ Finally, there may be a break in the wiring somewhere. Let a mechanic tackle this problem.

Aiming your headlights

Are your headlights pointing every which way except where they should? It's easy to check and adjust them. And if you'll be towing a trailer during the summer, you'll have to adjust your headlights to compensate; all that extra weight on the vehicle's rear end will make your headlights reach toward the stratosphere.

1. Find some flat pavement and a vertical surface such as your garage door. If you pull a trailer, adjust your headlights with it attached and loaded. Once it's dark enough for headlights to be seen, turn on the low beams and park about 1 foot from the door. Mark the center of each illuminated spot with masking tape.

Masking tape

2. Back up exactly 25 feet and park. Go to the garage door and examine where the center of each headlight is now located. The correct position of each light is 2 inches below and to the right of the tape strip. If your car has four headlights instead of two, the high beam should be centered on the tape.

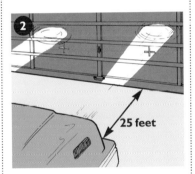

25 feet

3. Adjust the headlights by turning the vertical adjustment screw, located at the top of the headlight (you may have to remove some trim to uncover the screw), with a Phillips screwdriver.

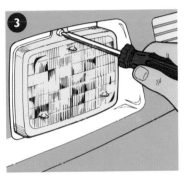

Another method (below) is to use a special aiming device you might find at an auto parts store. It allows you to adjust the headlights without having to use a long flat surface and a wall.

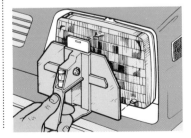

Ever wonder why oncoming drivers blink their lights at you? Maybe your misaimed lights are making *them* blink.

Lights and blinkers

Repairing a broken taillight lens

Crunch! You really didn't see that light pole you backed into in the parking lot, and now your taillight lens is broken. It probably won't seem like a big deal—until you price a replacement; some cost hundreds of dollars. Well, even if a chunk is missing, you can probably fix it.

If the lens is just cracked, glue it back together with a two-part epoxy or one of those instant glues. If a small piece is missing (below), cover the opening with lens repair tape, which costs less than $2 at most auto parts stores.

1. A better fix is to use Loctite's inexpensive Form-A-Lens repair kit. It's not a glue but a special plastic that closely matches the original lens. Take the lens off the vehicle. Then, if the missing chunk has numerous ridges and textures, use some modeling clay to make a mold of the area from one of the good lenses. If the broken piece is flat, skip the mold. Simply cover the area with the clear film supplied in the kit.

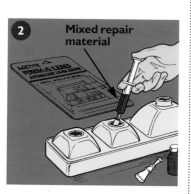
Mixed repair material

2. Clean the lens's surfaces, front and rear. Seal the opening from the front with either the clear film or the mold you made. Mix the repair material according to the directions, and fill the damaged area from the rear side of the lens. Allow it to dry overnight, peel away the film or mold, and you should have a lens that's as good as new.

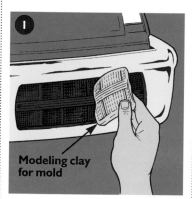
Modeling clay for mold

Lens tape

Back-up alarm

Do you live in a busy neighborhood where kids and pets abound? Is it hard to see behind the car as you back down the driveway? Get peace of mind by installing a back-up warning alarm. It will send out an audible alarm whenever your vehicle is put in reverse. Alarms cost about $20 at most auto parts stores.

Installation is easy. Remove the taillight lens assembly or pull the socket out of the lamp housing (you can usually get at the area through the trunk). Replace the standard bulb with the back-up alarm and bulb assembly.

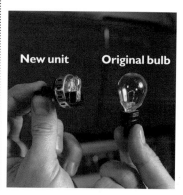
New unit   Original bulb

Dashboard electronics

Lights-on warning buzzer

How many times have you walked off, leaving the car's lights shining brightly . . . and the battery draining to zero? Don't you just hate that? Fortunately, there's an inexpensive solution: a warning buzzer that plugs into your fuse panel. Your local auto parts store and Radio Shack both sell these small 12-volt buzzers. Installation takes only minutes. Here's how to do it:

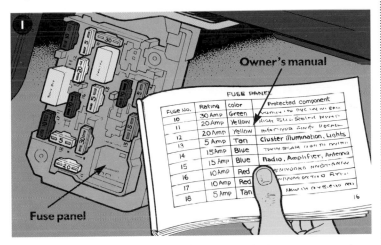

1. Find the fuse panel and identify the **fuse** for the instrument panel lights (the owner's manual or a diagram on the fuse panel will help). Temporarily connect the buzzer's red wire to this fuse. Now connect the white wire to any fuse that belongs to something that's turned on or off by the ignition, such as the radio.

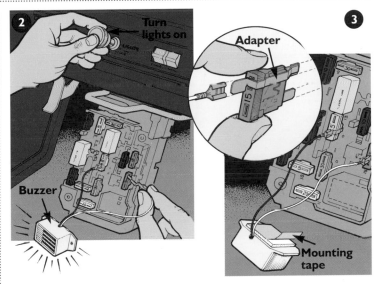

2. Test the buzzer by turning on the lights with the ignition still off. The buzzer should sound. Turning off the lights or turning on the ignition should silence the buzzer. If it doesn't, move the white wire to a different fuse.

3. Permanently connect both wires to the fuses, using the adapters supplied in the kit. Mount the buzzer on any nearby flat surface with the supplied foam tape.

It's so cheap you kinda wonder why every car doesn't have one.

Dashboard electronics

Jumping gauges

Needles on the temperature and gasoline gauges shouldn't jump beyond the *Hot* and *Full* marks when the engine certainly isn't hot and the gas tank is maybe only half full.

The reason for intermittent "gauge blimping," as automotive engineers call it, is a loose or defective electrical system ground wire. Have a technician check the instrument cluster ground wire that's usually attached to the dash panel. If this wire is loose, vibration can cause it to lose contact momentarily and make the gauges misbehave.

Then have the technician check the common ground connection. This is the place where various ground wires intersect (on a car, they're always black, not green as in a household system). This point could be on the **radiator** supports, the inner fender wells, or the **firewall**. The actual connection to the car may be a rather small screw or bolt—if it corrodes or loosens, grounding suffers and intermittent elec-

Needles to say, a gauge that lies to you is a hardly worth space on your dash.

trical problems are the result. Have the common ground disconnected, its connection cleaned, and the attachment hole on the sheet metal drilled out to ¼ inch. Then secure the ground wire with a bolt, nut, and locking washers to ensure it stays put.

Herky-jerky speedometer

A speedometer needle that wavers back and forth, accompanied by a loud and really annoying squeak at low speeds, probably means the speedometer cable is crying out for lubrication.

On older cars with cruise control and a two-piece cable, try lubricating the cable yourself. Auto parts stores sell speedometer cable lubricant in small tubes. Locate and unscrew the cables from the cruise unit, found on the left inner fender, and slowly add the lube to the housing. If this doesn't do the trick, take the car to your service station and have a mechanic remove the cable and lube it.

After removing the cable, your mechanic may find that it's kinked and can't be straightened; it will have to be replaced. It'll take about an hour to have the cable lubricated or about 90 minutes to have a new one installed.

Electrical miscellany

All the right stuff

The word on fuses

Your vehicle runs as much on electricity as it does on gasoline. Whenever the electricity quits flowing, the first place to check is the **fuse** panel. But be warned: A modern car can have twenty or more fuses. Sometimes temporary conditions cause a fuse to blow, so all you may need to do is replace the fuse. If it continues to blow, you have a short somewhere that must be tracked down.

It pays to buy a package of spare fuses and an appropriate puller. Usually the vehicle comes with only a few spares; they're probably lodged in the fuse-box cover or parked in extra, unwired spaces in the fuse box itself. Those few spares might not be enough to get you going again. (Never use a fuse that's a different amperage from the original.)

There are four common types of automotive fuses: the flat plug style in both regular and mini-plug types (the mini-plug fits better in the crowded fuse panels typical of newer cars); the familiar glass cylinder; and a look-alike glass cylinder design that has thick, pointed ends and is most common on European models.

Some pullers also include a fuse tester to ensure the problem

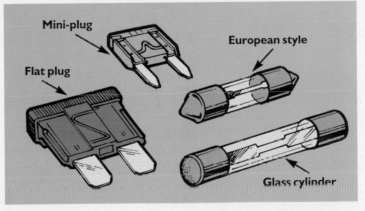

Mini-plug

European style

Flat plug

Glass cylinder

is indeed the fuse. The price for all this trip- and hassle-saving gear? About $5 to $10, and it will all fit easily into a corner of your glove compartment.

When checking fuses, remove them and hold them up to a light. That's the best way to tell if the thin fusible element has really melted.

Safety light

One of the most important, yet least expensive, safety devices ever invented for passenger cars is the center-mounted brake light. Mounted in the rear window, the light significantly improves brake light visibility from behind and has been effective in reducing rear-end collisions.

Adding a third brake light to an older vehicle is an easy DIY project. Kits are available at your local auto parts store. On sedans, the light is attached to the rear package shelf (or to a pedestal if the package shelf is well below the rear glass). On hatchbacks and station wagons, it simply attaches to the glass with adhesive. Wiring is straightforward; just follow the instructions in the kit.

Three's a crowd, but the third one saves plenty of lives.

Electrical miscellany

Alternate choice

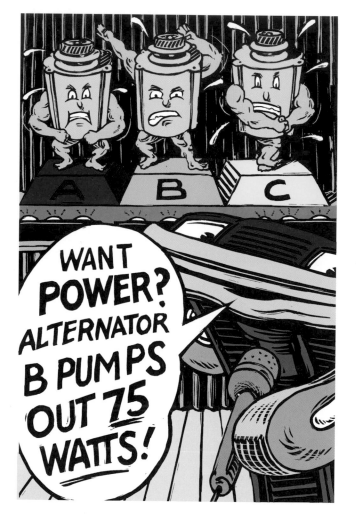

WANT POWER? ALTERNATOR B PUMPS OUT 75 WATTS!

When the battery seems weak and the "Service Engine Soon" light comes on, your technician might suspect a problem with the charging system. One of the first things to suspect is the **alternator**.

Until the early 1970's, cars used **generators** to supply the electrical needs of a running car. A generator produces direct current (DC), but not enough to keep up with all the electrical needs of modern cars (everything from cellular phones to CD players and fog lamps). Alternators are now standard because they produce alternating current (AC), which can be converted into all the DC current your car will ever need.

Sometimes when an electrical problem seems related to the alternator, a mechanic will simply replace the unit. If problems crop up again soon, however, maybe it's not the alternator's fault.

Check for a loose fan belt first—it drives the alternator as well as the fan. If the "Service Engine Soon" light is coming on, it could be that the engine wiring harness is being rubbed through and bare wires are coming into contact with metal. But why, then, does the problem go away for a while after a new alternator is installed? That's probably because the technician has to move the wiring harness to install the new alternator. In time, though, vibration causes the harness to shift back again.

If the alternator is charging properly, there's no short circuit in the wiring, and all connections are tight including those at the starter motor, then the alternator is the problem after all. It just isn't able to replenish the electrical draw on the battery from all the high-powered goodies you have in the car. Discuss with your mechanic the practicality of installing a higher-amperage alternator. Maybe the increased capacity will keep your car from electrical starvation.

Replacing a broken power antenna mast

It's easy to damage or break a power antenna mast. Leave the stereo on as you go through the automatic car wash and you'll get to watch the brushes and rollers as they bend, fold, and mutilate the mast. Replacing just the mast is easy and relatively inexpensive on most cars. On Chryslers, Fords, and many imports, the mast is replaceable without removing and disassembling the whole power antenna unit. Most GM vehicles require that the entire power antenna unit be removed, a job best left to a professional.

1. Extend the mast as far as it will go by turning on the radio or flipping up the antenna switch. When the motor stops, unscrew the top nut on the antenna body and manually collapse the mast as much as possible to expose the geared drive cable. Note which direction the cable teeth face. Now drive the cable up and out of

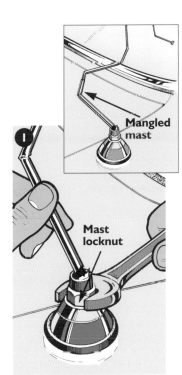

Mangled mast

Mast locknut

the unit until the gear teeth disengage by turning the antenna switch off, then on again. Don't pull the cable while the motor is running; wait for it to release, then lift out the assembly.

2. Reverse the process to install the new mast. Insert the new cable through the top nut, slide the nut to the top of the mast, then feed the cable into the unit, with the gear teeth facing in the proper direction, until it stops. Turn off the radio or flip the antenna switch down. As the cable teeth engage the motor drive, feed the cable and then the mast into the opening.

Once the motor stops, tighten the top nut. As a final test, turn the radio or antenna switch on to fully extend the mast, then off to fully retract it.

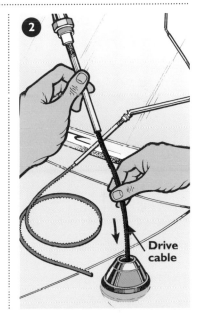

Drive cable

Quick tip
Electrical tape wrap

When you have to wrap wires with electrical tape in a tight area, pull off a few inches of tape and wrap it loosely on itself around your index finger so the sticky side is out. Then you can roll the tape around the wire with your thumb, using your middle finger to support it.

Sticky side out

Lookin' Good (Inside and Out)

Taking care of your car or truck is a hallowed tradition, and for good reason.

Whether you do everything yourself or have some of it done for you, the basic rule is that if you treat your vehicles well, they'll reward you at trade-in time (and be more trouble-free meanwhile). Besides, you'll be a lot happier driving a clean, prepped, and comfortable car, won't you?

The best part is that you can do almost all of this stuff yourself with a truly minimal investment of both time and tools. A Saturday morning, maybe a little help from the kids even, and you're set—you can even remove those pesky dealership emblems if you want to. Still, an understanding of what works and what doesn't never hurts, and if it saves you some time, hey, there's lots you can do with that!

Wash, wax, and touch-ups

How to wash a car

Proper and frequent washing is the first step in protecting your car's finish. Unfortunately, you're probably doing it wrong. Let's see. You just grab a bucket, a hose, and the dish detergent or laundry soap, and then, with the car parked in the sun, go merrily to work. Right?

First of all, household detergents are far too harsh for automotive finishes. They not only strip any existing wax from the finish but also tend to dry the paint itself, sapping the life right out and leaving it more vulnerable to the elements. Second, you should never wash the car in direct sun because you'll end up with a spotted surface, and because cold water hosed onto a hot surface can create microscopic cracks in the finish. But hey, don't feel bad—you got the bucket part right.

Always wash your vehicle with a product specifically formulated for automotive finishes. You'll find plenty of these products on the store shelves right alongside automotive waxes and polishes. Automotive washes thoroughly clean the finish and minimize spotting as the vehicle dries.

Start with a cool car. Scrub the tires and wheels first, using cleaners specially formulated not to harm their finish. Flush the

Have bucket. Will travel.

bucket to remove residue and dirt, then fill it with cool water and the right amount of car-wash soap. Don't use too much soap; it'll be difficult to rinse off and will leave a hazy film. Next, rinse the car to remove the heavy dirt. Then soap it with a soft, clean brush, sponge, or cloth designed specifically for car finishes. Rinse again, and dry the finish with a clean terry-cloth towel or a chamois. Doesn't it look great?

Convertible-top care

So you finally bought that shiny new convertible. How do you care for the top?

✔ **Keep it clean.** Wash the top regularly with car-wash detergent, not laundry or dish soap. Don't wax the top or rear window—any type of wax will draw the oils out of the vinyl fabric.

✔ **Keep it healthy.** Apply a vinyl protectant to the top after each wash. Not only does this restore the shine, it extends the top's life by replacing the polymers drawn out by sunlight.

✔ **Mind the rear window.** The soft plastic rear window is easily scratched, so avoid scrubbing it with a brush or sponge. Just flush the window with fresh water.

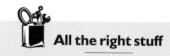 **All the right stuff**

A chamois is mutton special

Chamois has been used by professional auto detailers for years. Made from high-quality tanned sheepskin, chamois is soft and super-absorbent; it can dry a car without streaking or spotting, leaving a sparkling shine that makes this high-priced item worth every penny. Simply rinse the chamois in clean water, wring it to remove excess moisture, then drag it over a wet car to "pull off" the water. You can get synthetic chamois (at about half the price), but there's nothing better than the real McCoy.

Understanding car waxes

There's a lot of confusion and more than a little mystique surrounding the subject of car waxes. For example, maybe you think that because it's an old car, wax won't help. Or because your car sports a high-tech finish, you don't have to wax it. Or that "natural" waxes are superior to synthetics. Well, here's the truth about how to buy right.

Why bother? Wax protects your car's finish. Paint is under constant attack from the environment, and over time that glossy surface erodes and oxidizes, becoming dull and rough. Better paints make the finish on modern cars shinier and more durable. The basecoat/clearcoat system offered by auto makers on most of their models protects the pigmented colorcoat with an extra layer of clear resin that adds depth to the shine. But don't believe anyone who calls this a "no-wax" finish (see p. 136).

Understanding waxes. It seems like there are 13 bizillion types of waxes on the store shelves, so how do you decide which to buy? Simple: Take a look at your car, analyze the condition of the paint, and follow these guidelines:

✔ If it's a new car and the paint is still in near-perfect condition, use a polysealer or a nonabrasive pure wax intended for clearcoat finishes.

✔ After a year or so of exposure, a car's finish will have oxidized to some degree. At this point, a cleaner/wax is usually the way to go. These products include solvents and powders to strip old wax, remove road film, and completely clean the surface of the paint. They restore the shine by removing oxidized paint and smoothing the remaining surface, but they're milder than polishing or rubbing compounds.

Most cleaner/waxes are formulated to work on clearcoat finishes. Properly used, they leave a protective layer of wax on a perfectly clean surface, not a layer of paste on top of old wax, road tar, and oxidized paint.

✔ If the finish is dull and weathered, then a finish restorer or polishing compound/rubbing compound may revive it (see p.135).

New car or clunker, there's a "just right" wax to give it showroom shine.

✔ Be particularly careful in choosing a product for vehicles with a clearcoat finish. Too much abrasive in the wax will scratch the top layer of clear paint, giving a dulled appearance. That's the logic behind the new nonabrasive car waxes. You can feel the abrasiveness of a product by rubbing some between two fingers. If it feels gritty, it's very abrasive.

Natural waxes, such as carnauba, form a water-shedding barrier on top of the paint. Thus, most of us measure the success of our waxing by how well water beads on the surface. Most synthetic products use a combination of natural waxes and silicone polymers. The silicones add slickness, shine, and durability to the finish, while the wax provides the water-shedding protection. The natural slipperiness of the silicones also reduces the chance of scratching the paint during the washing process, whether it be by hand or at an automatic car wash.

✔ Generally, liquids are easier and faster to apply than pastes, but the greater effort involved in applying a paste usually results in a cleaner, more uniform finish.

Wash, wax, and touch-ups

How to wax a car

Obey the first waxing commandment or the wax will become almost impossible to remove (and may stain the finish): **Thou shalt never ever apply wax to a hot surface or in direct sunlight.** After that, though, the rest is easy.

Start by washing and drying the car. Check for any specific instructions on the wax can, but generally you'll have to dampen an applicator to apply the wax. If no applicator is supplied, an old T-shirt that's been washed many times makes a great applicator. Apply a very light, even coat of wax to a small section at a time. Let it dry to a haze and then wipe it off with a clean soft, dry cloth; then lightly buff the surface. For buffing nothing beats a pure cotton baby diaper. The longer wax sits on the finish, the more difficult it becomes to remove.

Applying wax with an electric buffer seems to promise better results with less effort, particularly if you have other things to do with your weekend. It can indeed do a nice job, but if you put a bit too much pressure on it or pause slightly too long in one place, you can easily burn the paint or scratch a clearcoat finish. So if you plan to swap elbow grease for electric power, just do it carefully. Read the label of the wax can to see if it has a minimum or maximum **RPM** recommended for power buffing. Many products come with these ratings.

Some people like to use a spray wax, feeling that it goes on easier than paste or liquid. Maybe so, but to avoid spraying wax onto the windows you'll end up pouring it onto a cloth first anyway, reducing the speed advantage of spray wax.

If you can't quite buff off all the wax residue, ask at an auto parts store for a product that will finish the job. Your reward will be a car with a show-car shine.

Lax about wax

You put on the wax and took a snooze, didn't you? Well, there's a big job in your future: baked-on wax doesn't come off easily. To remedy the situation, buy a clean soft sponge (the kind that are sold in photo supply shops work best), saturate it with liquid laundry detergent, and rub down a small section of the body. Don't let the detergent dry or you'll have even more of a mess. Immediately hose down the area with lots of water, and move on to the next section. If this doesn't work, try an automotive wax remover, sold at auto parts stores. Be careful, though, because this stuff can damage the paint if not used correctly. After you get the wax off, you may have to use a finish restorer to help get the shine back.

Restoring faded paint

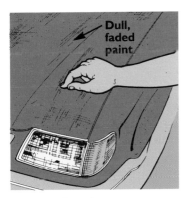

Dull, faded paint

Does the paint on your car look dull and dirty even after a washing? Sunlight and road grime cause the paint to oxidize, creating the dull film. Rub your finger firmly across the paint. If some of the color shows on your finger, the paint has aged past salvation and repainting is the only option. But if no color shows, you can probably revive the paint with an abrasive polish. Here's how:

1. Using a soft, clean cloth (a cloth diaper is perfect), buff a small area with a cleaner/polish that is mildly abrasive. If that produces good results, continue around the car, switching to fresh sections of cloth frequently.

Mildly abrasive cleaner/polish

Beware of claims made by some finish restorers. By adding color pigment to their products, they aim to "revitalize" your faded paint, but they may actually discolor it. Of course, if the finish is totally ruined anyway, this stuff may just be for you.

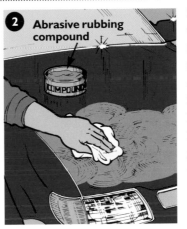

Abrasive rubbing compound

COMPOUND

2. Heavy oxidation in areas such as the hood or roof may require a more abrasive polish. From least to most abrasive, there are the liquid cleaner/polishes, then paste polishing compounds, and finally paste hand-rubbing compounds. Use the least abrasive product that does the job. With the more abrasive products, you must be careful not to remove too much paint.

Paste wax

LJW 922

3. When you've restored the shine, apply one coat of a good paste wax to protect the paint—but only one coat. Applying two coats is a waste of time and energy; when you apply the second coat you'll wipe off the first one.

Wash, wax, and touch-ups

Getting rid of paint swirl

Swirl marks in a clearcoat paint finish dull the finish, which is suppose to make paint shine like a diamond. Here's how to remove these unsightly marks.

Start by treating the finish with a mild polishing compound—note the words "mild" and "polishing." Don't use rubbing compound; it's too abrasive. Professionals like products that don't contain wax or silicone. Be sure to follow the directions to the letter, because if you misuse the compound you'll rub off a lot of the car's paint. Bad idea.

Use an oscillating buffer to apply the polishing compound. This neat little device is very reasonably priced, but you can also rent one at your local tool rental place. Believe it or not, compound is speed-sensitive, meaning that the buffer must be used at a specific RPM if you want the best results.

Going too fast will overheat the finish, staining it or causing blemishes. Buffing too slowly may just cause more scratches. You might want to experiment on an unobtrusive part of the car first before you start in on the rest of it.

Follow this by applying glazing. Again, following the directions is a must.

Finally, to prevent swirl marks in the first place, have the car washed only at a brushless carwash place; better yet, do it yourself. At home use soft clean cloths to wash, dry, and wax your car. Don't use a rotary buffer when you wax or polish your car—it's seldom needed to get a good wax job on a clearcoat paint finish.

Treating milky-white red paint

Red paint on the hood, roof, or trunk of your car may be turning milky white, but don't blame acid rain; blame sunlight. The problem is called "chalking," and it's a natural aging process. Red paint contains a lot of yellow pigment, so it fades faster than many other colors.

An auto detailer should be able to tell you if treating the car with professional-grade rubbing compound (the most abrasive compound of all) will remove chalked paint and still leave a paint film thick enough to protect the car. If there's no detailing pro in your area, ask someone at the best body shop. To reduce chalking in the first place, wash your car often to remove chemical contaminants that lie on the paint (the reason horizontal surfaces chalk first), and try to park your car in the shade.

 **Bob says . . .**

Get the lowdown on clearcoats

I'd like to clear up some confusion. A clearcoat finish is a crystal-clear coating applied to auto paint while it's still wet. Does "clearcoat" mean "no-wax?" Nope. It's simply paint with the pigment left out, so it still needs a protective layer of wax.

But wax this stuff too soon and you'll destroy the finish. I recommend that you wait 3 to 6 months before waxing a damaged area that has been repainted, but it's OK to wax your *new* car after a month. Why? Clearcoat applied by the dealer is baked on with heat lamps and can take a while to cure completely. The factory uses equipment that bakes the finish a lot more thoroughly.

Restoring clearcoat finishes

Protective "clearcoat" finishes have been around for a while now. Essentially a layer of clear paint over the colored paint, clearcoat provides added depth and protection to the auto's finish. But over time, the clearcoat can dull. Here's how to restore it.

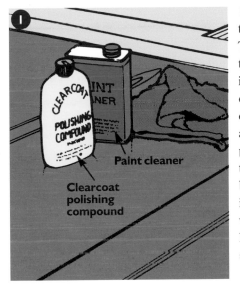

Paint cleaner

Clearcoat polishing compound

1. Wash your vehicle thoroughly, and dry it. Then carefully evaluate the finish. If the clearcoat is clouded or hazy but not otherwise damaged, try either a "paint cleaner" or a clearcoat polishing compound. Make sure the latter one is specifically labeled "clear-coat polishing compound," but whether it's a paste or a liquid is a matter of personal preference.

When the sun shines, beaded acid rain can magnify it and etch the clearcoat; hose off the car with fresh water after a rain!

2. Wet a small section of the car with the paint cleaner or polishing compound. Rub in straight lines with either a clean folded cotton diaper, a terry-cloth towel, or a special knitted polishing cloth (you can get one for a few dollars at an auto parts store). Don't rub in a circular motion, which will just create swirl marks that you'll have to remove again.

Rub back and forth

3. Buff the section clean when the polish hazes over. Use either a new cloth or a clean portion of the old cloth. Repeat the process for the rest of the car, working a small area at a time and rubbing only in a straight line. When you're done, apply a coat of good-quality wax to protect the newly restored finish.

Wash, wax, and touch-ups

Cleaning trim

Sometimes as you wax your car, the wax dries on plastic bumpers and moldings, discoloring them. Try this to safely remove the spots:

First try a potion of baking soda and mineral spirits, which won't harm these plastic parts. Mix the two to make a soupy paste. Apply the compound to the entire bumper or length of molding—if you don't, the portion you treat will appear brighter than the rest. On textured bumpers and trim, use a plastic-bristle brush to get into the crevices (an old toothbrush works great). Rub as hard as you can. Use a fresh Turkish towel rag to remove the cleaner while it's still wet. (Don't let it dry, or you'll have to repeat the whole process.)

If one application doesn't work, give it another and still another before trying the commercial (and more caustic) wax and grease removers available from auto parts stores. If you end up using one of the commercial critters, carefully follow the directions on the can and be extra-sure you wipe it off while it's still wet. More than one application may be needed.

After you remove the stains, apply a light coat of trim protectant, such as Armor All. Put the protectant on a rag first so you'll have better control applying it. Remove the protectant immediately if any gets on the car's finish. These compounds will stain the finish and are as stubborn as sap to get off once dry.

One final piece of advice: Whichever cleaning agent you use, keep the car out of the sunlight as you work.

All the right stuff

Keep those tires black

Tires should be black, not dingy brown or gray. To keep them shiny and black after you wash the car, periodically apply a tire dressing and protectant. Besides keeping the tires looking good for many moons, the product also forms a protective barrier on your tires. Tires exposed to prolonged sunlight, road salts, and other chemical compounds can begin to deteriorate. By sealing the tires with either silicone- or rubber-based compounds, you are protecting the rubber against damage that can cause the side walls to crack (this unsightly condition is called *dry rot* in the auto biz). Just be sure not to get the stuff on the treads because it can interfere with steering and braking.

Scratch repair

Manufacturing I.D. plate

To fix a scratch, start with some information. Find your vehicle's manufacturing information (a decal or metal plate attached to the driver's doorjamb, under the hood, in the glove compartment, or attached to the spare tire cover), which specifies the paint color code. Then use the code to buy a bottle of matching touch-up paint from your dealer or an auto parts store. If there's rust on the car, you'll also need primer or a liquid rust converter. If your vehicle has a clearcoat finish, buy that as well. Now you can get to work.

1. Clean the scratch and the immediate area around it with soap and water or with mineral spirits. Let it dry thoroughly. Paint won't adhere properly unless the area is perfectly clean and rust-free.

2. Mask the surrounding area. If the scratch has any rust, it must be removed or neutralized (if there's no rust, go to the next step). Remove the rust with fine steel wool (wrap a small piece around the eraser end of a pencil) or use a rust converter, which chemically transforms the rust into a paintable surface. Apply the converter with an artist's brush.

2 Rust converter

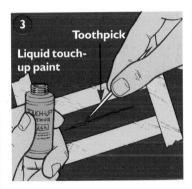

3 Liquid touch-up paint Toothpick

3. Mix the paint thoroughly, and apply it with either the supplied brush, a toothpick, or an artist's brush. Apply in one direction only and take your time. Don't let the paint build up higher than the surrounding surface. If the car has a clearcoat finish, apply the clear touchup after the paint dries.

4. Wait several days for the paint to dry thoroughly; then use polishing compound to blend the painted area in with the surrounding finish. Finally, wash and wax the car to protect both the new and the old paint.

4 POLISHING COMPOUND

Wash, wax, and touch-ups

Cleaning under the hood

A clean engine runs cooler and is more fuel-efficient. But the bad ol' days of spraying on a powerful solvent and washing the grime down onto the ground are long gone. Here's how to clean under the hood with minimal impact on the environment:

✔ Do it only when there's a large buildup of grease and grime.

✔ Professional engine-cleaning outfits are set up to dispose of the waste properly—you can find them in the phone book.

✔ If you're going to do it yourself, use a water-based, biodegradable, nontoxic, all-purpose cleaner such as Simple Green or Permatex Enviro-Safe Cleaner & Degreaser.

✔ Use as little of the cleaner as possible.

✔ Position a large drip pan under the engine to catch the oily grime. Let it dry out in the pan; then dispose of it in the trash.

✔ After you're done, lubricate the hood bumpers, hinges, and hood latch with lithium grease.

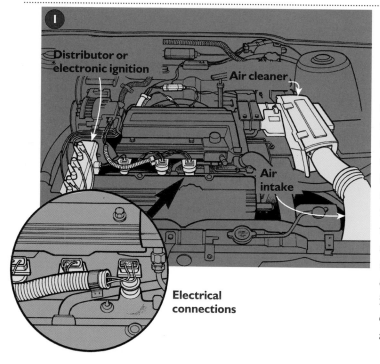

1. Identify areas that must not be cleaned. Wiring connections, any electronic components, and the air cleaner and its intake are the key worry spots. These areas must be sealed. Your owner's manual may identify others, but cover whatever you aren't sure about.

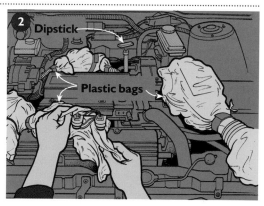

2. Spray the distributor cap, coil, and plug wires with a light coat of moisture-displacing spray lubricant or a similar lubricant. Then cover vulnerable engine components with plastic bags secured with tape and rubber bands. Put plastic drop cloths on the cowl (the grille at the base of the windshield) and both fenders to protect the paint against spotting and overspray, and you're ready to work (facing page).

Plastic over cowl

Cleaner

Plastic drop cloths taped in place

Drain pan

3. Work outdoors, with a cool engine, and wear eye protection.
Put a drain pan under the engine. Remove any heavy grease buildup with a putty knife. Apply the cleaner according to the instructions, and wash it off using medium water pressure. Use as little water as possible, rinsing from the top down. *Don't* use a pressure washer and *don't* spray water directly onto any electrical wires, oil fill caps, or dipsticks. Then remove the plastic covers from the engine components (but not the cowl or fenders), start the engine, and let it idle for 10 to 15 minutes to dry out completely.

Zapping sap

Tree sap sticks like glue when it falls on a car. If left alone, it can bake on and stain or blemish the finish. It will also ruin wiper inserts. Here's the fix:

✔Hold a plastic spatula against sap lumps; push to break 'em off.

✔Mix laundry detergent into really hot water. Wearing heavy rubber gloves to avoid a burn, dip a soft cloth into the sudsy solution and rub the residue as hard as you can. Repeat until the sap disappears.

✔Thoroughly hose down the area with cold water.

✔Though it's time-consuming, scrub all the windows carefully. If enough sap gets stuck on glass, it can cause a roll-down window to jump its track.

✔After the metal dries, polish the spots that had sap on them with auto-body polish; then wax the whole car to protect it.

Wash, wax, and touch-ups

Removing decals and dealer emblems

Removing old decals, bumper stickers, and similar stuff without damaging the paint is easy if you know how. Some will come off with ease after you squirt them with a spray lubricant or a similar product. If that doesn't work, try this:

Bumper sticker circa 1960

Hair dryer

I. The best method is to use a hand-held hair dryer or heat gun to soften the adhesive so you can peel the decal away. If you use a heat gun, be careful not to use too much heat.

2. Dealer emblems (don't you hate those things!) are often tougher to remove than decals. For this you need something to pry with that won't damage the paint. Try either a plastic kitchen spatula or a wide putty knife with the blade covered with duct tape. After warming the area with the hair dryer or heat gun, carefully work the spatula or putty knife under the emblem and then pry it up.

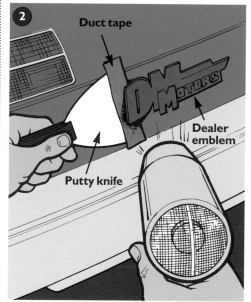

Duct tape

Dealer emblem

Putty knife

Old adhesive residue

RUBBING ALCOHOL

Rubbing alcohol

3. Dampen a soft, clean cloth with rubbing alcohol (or with tar remover intended for auto finishes) and wipe away any remaining adhesive. Rub gently. Really stubborn residue can usually be removed with finger friction or by scraping it with your fingernail. Because the alcohol removes wax, buff the area with polishing compound, and then apply a fresh coat of wax.

Restoring the black to trim

Even though your car's black plastic parts may have faded to a dull gray by now, with a little work and the right products you can bring back the luster and shine. High-gloss black and painted body-color trim can be waxed and buffed just like any other bodywork, but textured plastic trim needs special attention. Here's how to treat it:

2. Once clean, the luster can be restored with multiple applications of Armor All or similar protectant. Spray the stuff on a clean rag and rub it into the trim; then buff off the excess. Do this several times; yes, this is a lot of work, but it's necessary.

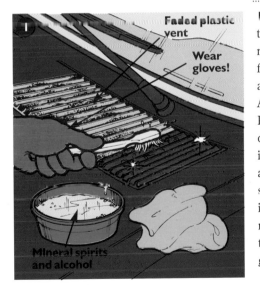

1. Remove any faded residue that whitish blight that seems to resist virtually all washing efforts—with an old toothbrush and a liberal amount of Armor All or similar vinyl protectant. Really stubborn spots may require a 70:30 mix of mineral spirits and rubbing alcohol. Because alcohol can permanently dull some plastics, first test the mix in a small, less visible spot. This mixture is potent, so keep it off the car's finish and wear rubber gloves when applying it.

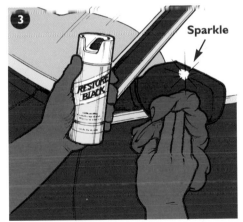

3. Finally, top off the trim with a specialty product like Black Chrome, Meguiar's Vinyl & Rubber Cleaner, Black Again, or 3M's Scotchgard Protective Gel. Repeated applications of these products over several weeks will provide a deep, long-lasting luster.

Bodywork

The saga of sagging doors

Car door hard to shut and lock? Does it seem to sag when you open it? It may be out of alignment. Open the door slightly, holding it almost closed against the striker (the mushroom-shaped metal post on the car body). Did the edge of the door drop a bit as it opened? Repeat the latching/opening sequence a few times to be sure. If the door drops slightly, it's probably sagging. Here's how to confirm your suspicion and correct the problem.

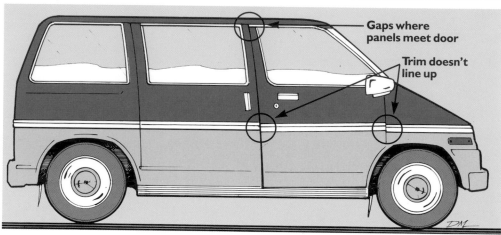

Gaps where panels meet door

Trim doesn't line up

Obvious sag or misalignment

1. Make a visual check: With the door fully closed, stand back about 10 feet and look at the door's alignment with the rest of the body. Do the chrome trim pieces or body lines (where panels meet) match perfectly? They should.

2. Try making minor adjustments by fitting a 2x2 wood block above or below the lower hinge to act as a wedge between the door and the body, then . . .

Door hinge

Wood block

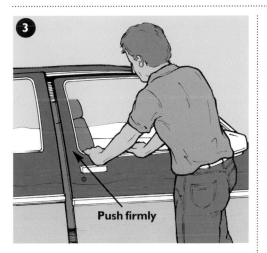

3

Push firmly

3. From the outside, push firmly on the door (with the 2x2 still in place) to gently bend the lower hinge. Recheck the door's fit after every try. Bend the hinge just enough to restore alignment—no more. This calls for care, because you don't want to make the problem worse by overbending the hinge.

If the doors don't fit, your car will feel like a clunker even if it isn't one.

4. If the sag is so severe that bending the hinge doesn't correct it, you may have to loosen the hinge mounting bolts for a larger range of adjustment. It sounds simple, but it's possible to really mess things up, so you'll probably be better off letting a professional do the work. If you do attempt it, support the bottom of the door (it's very heavy) on a cushioned jack stand or crate. Scribe alignment marks with a screwdriver or awl around each hinge before loosening any bolts; then loosen and adjust one hinge a tiny bit at a time. Recheck the alignment after each adjustment.

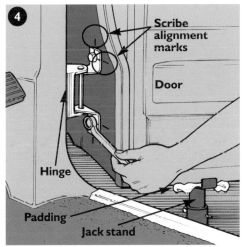

4

Scribe alignment marks

Door

Hinge

Padding

Jack stand

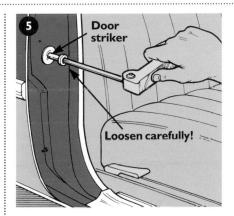

5

Door striker

Loosen carefully!

5. If bending the hinge (Steps 2 and 3) corrected most of the misalignment, you can get things perfect by adjusting the fit between the latch and the striker. With the proper wrench (you'll find Torx, Allen, Posidrive, and regular hex bolts being used—your auto parts store will have a wrench that fits), carefully loosen the striker just enough so it can be moved. Slide the striker up or down, in or out, until the door latches properly. Then retighten. Be very, *very* careful to not loosen the bolt too much, or the retaining nut will fall off and disappear inside the vehicle's bodywork and you'll have a major repair problem.

Bodywork

Fixing loose trim

Loose trim is more than unsightly and annoying—if it suddenly falls off into the path of a following car, the resulting evasive actions could lead to an accident. Keep that trim where it belongs; here's how.

1. Don't glue it! Although it's tempting to reattach a loose section of body trim or door molding with glue, don't do it. It's messy and probably won't hold long. Instead, once the trim begins to separate from the panel, peel it the rest of the way off so you can properly reattach it.

2. Dampen a clean rag with an adhesive remover (it'll cost a few dollars at an auto parts store), and carefully clean off all adhesive on the back of the trim. You may have to use adhesive remover to help lift the trim where the adhesive is still strong. Once the trim is off, carefully clean the surface of the body panel where the trim goes, being careful not to damage the paint.

Rubber gloves

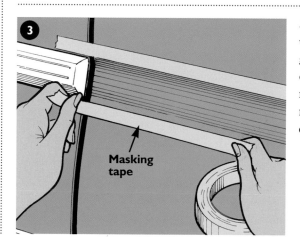

Masking tape

3. Apply one or two strips of masking tape to the body panel to serve as a guide for reattaching the trim. Use other pieces of trim or body lines as reference points in order to get the masking tape on straight, then proceed with next step.

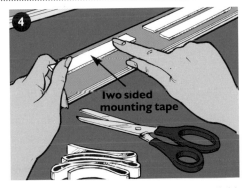

4. Attach special two-sided mounting tape (it's available at auto parts stores) to the back side of the trim. For wide moldings, you may have to use two side-by-side strips of tape. Before peeling away the backing paper, hold the molding against the body panel to see if a single layer of tape is thick enough to ensure solid contact with the panel. In some cases, a double thickness of tape will be necessary.

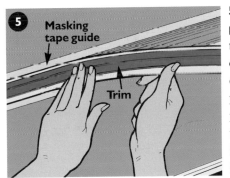

5. Peel off the backing paper, and using the masking tape as a guide, carefully center and align one end of the molding, pressing it firmly into place. Then work down the length of the molding, aligning and pressing it into place.

Rustproofing? Who needs it!

Does aftermarket rustproofing actually prevent rust? Properly applied, yes. Does your new car need it? Probably not. For one thing, the contracts are filled with loopholes that minimize the rustproofer's liability. Also, only outer body panels are covered (not the floor pan), and only for rust through (not surface rust). And if you're likely to replace the vehicle within 5 years, you'll probably never make a claim anyway.

If you *do* go for it, the best-quality jobs involve drilling holes so the rustproofing can be delivered to every nook and cranny of the car.

Quick tip

Door won't close?

On the edge of a door there's a rotating latch with a pair of prongs. If accidentally flipped to the "closed" position, the door won't close no matter how hard you slam it. To fix the latch, simply lift the door handle as if to open the door. This should cause the latch to rotate to its "open" position. If it doesn't, hold the door handle open and rotate the latch downward with a screwdriver.

Interior tune-ups

Squishy carpets?

Water leaking into the car can be frustrating and annoying. After you mop it up, pull out a hair dryer and try to finish the work. Then put your Sherlock Holmes hat on and figure out what happened.

✔ Water leaking into the car at one spot can travel along electrical conduit and wander to the other side of the car—the stuff is really sneaky! But a good body shop mechanic shouldn't have any trouble locating and sealing the source of the leak. Let the sealer set up for a few days before running your car through the car wash. The high-pressure water nozzles used in some car washes can loosen fresh sealer and ruin the repair.

✔ If the carpeting isn't wet from rain, suspect the air conditioner. Run it for a few days, then feel the carpet. If it's wet again, blame the evaporator drain for allowing condensation to back up and drip into the passenger area. Maybe the drain tube is clogged; maybe it fell off. The tube comes down from behind the engine on the passenger side. It can be cleaned out or replaced.

✔ When you mop up any leak, check first to make sure it's not **coolant** leaking from the heater core or hoses. If it's greenish yellow (soak it up with a white paper towel) and has a sweet smell, it's coolant. Better take the car in for professional service.

✔ After the leak has been repaired, you may have to have the carpet removed so it can dry thoroughly. In some cases, the jute (cloth) backing of the carpet may be so damaged that you'll have to replace the carpet to eliminate a foul moldy smell inside the car.

Musty somethin'

You left the windows open last week, didn't you? And it rained, didn't it? That musty odor you now smell is bacteria thriving in lots of damp places. This is not a simple or cheap repair, so call your insurance company to see if you're covered. If not, have a carpet-cleaning company steam-clean the car's interior to kill the bacteria. The seats, carpet and carpet underpad must be removed, the floor pan washed with disinfectant, and the old carpet underpad discarded for a new one. The door trim and headliner may also have to be cleaned. The seats and carpet should be treated with an industrial-strength disinfectant before reinstallation.

If any power-operated accessories got wet (like the power window switches), dry them with compressed air; then spray them with electrical contact cleaner to keep the contacts from corroding.

Quick tip
Mini-shnoz

Trying to vacuum all those tiny nooks and crannies around the the dash? Try this goofy little tool. Poke a large plastic straw through the bottom of a stiff paper cup (a flexible straw works best), and run a bit of caulk around the straw. Just plunk the cap on the end of your vacuum hose and suction will hold it in place.

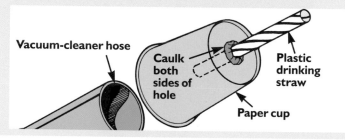

Vacuum-cleaner hose

Caulk both sides of hole

Plastic drinking straw

Paper cup

Fixing carpet burns

Someone's stray cigarette burned a hole in your car's carpet? Twenty minutes of work will repair the damage so that no one will ever know it happened.

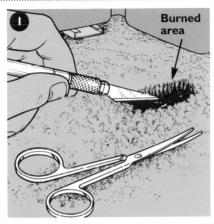

Burned area

1. Use a knife and small scissors to cut away all of the burned fibers and to scrape the blackened area clean.

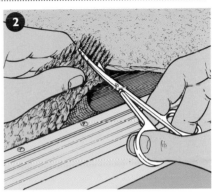

2. Cut enough carpet fibers to fill the hole. Take them from any hidden section of carpeting, such as from under a seat or doorsill (the sill is normally held in place by only a couple of screws).

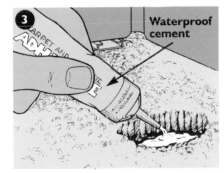

Waterproof cement

3. Dab a small amount of clear waterproof cement into the center of the burned spot.

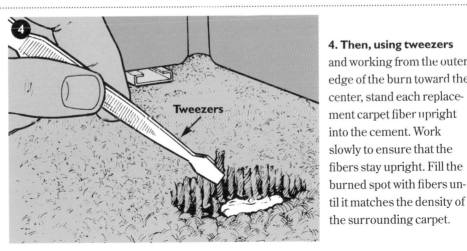

Tweezers

4. Then, using tweezers and working from the outer edge of the burn toward the center, stand each replacement carpet fiber upright into the cement. Work slowly to ensure that the fibers stay upright. Fill the burned spot with fibers until it matches the density of the surrounding carpet.

Interior tune-ups

Fixing tears in vinyl

Tools needed

Argh! You accidentally tore the vinyl seat in your car, right where everyone will see it. Now you can watch it grow until the split ruins the whole seat. Well, it's easy to fix if you tackle it right away. You'll need masking tape cut into thin strips, a razor knife or scissors, some glue applicators (toothpicks, thin cardboard, matches), and most important, a good-quality plastic/vinyl cement. It will cost only a few dollars at your auto parts store.

1. Draw the torn edges together, using thin strips of masking tape to hold them in place. Leave gaps for glue application. There are two secrets to a successful vinyl repair: (1) use the least amount of cement possible—better too little than too much, and (2) match the torn edges back together perfectly. Too much glue or misaligned edges will give you a messy, all-too-noticeable repair.

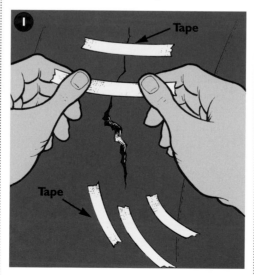

Tape

Tape

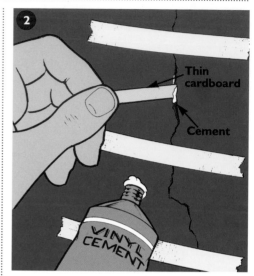

Thin cardboard

Cement

2. Put a drop or two of cement on a thin strip of cardboard, a toothpick, or a match. Slide the applicator and cement along the length of the tear, spreading the cement evenly. Take your time—patience will produce an almost invisible repair. Keep the glue off the masking tape, or remove the tape temporarily while you apply the glue and then reattach the tape. Let the cement dry overnight and then carefully peel off the tape. Repeat as necessary until all the edges of the tear are glued down.

Sagging headliners

A car's headliner (the insulating material over your head) needn't be replaced if it starts to sag. Headliners consist of foam-backed cloth glued to a molded fiberglass panel. In time the adhesive may lose its grip, but you can reattach the material by removing the headliner from the car, separating the material from the fiberglass panel, gently cleaning the parts with solvent-based cleaner on a rag, and re-gluing them together. It sounds like a whole bunch of work, but really, it's not that bad. You'll probably be done in less than an hour.

For an adhesive, you should use what the pros use—contact cement—but if that sounds too messy you can give double-sided tape a try, or a special spray adhesive made for reattaching trim. You can even use Velcro. Look for a "headliner repair kit" at your auto parts store.

Back to cement. Spread con-tact cement on the panel and on the foam backing. When the cement has dried on both parts, place the cloth/foam material on the panel, but don't press it down

until you've shifted it into posi tion—once it's down, it's down to stay. When the material and the panel are in line, firmly press them together, working from the center toward the edges to pre-vent wrinkles. That's all there is to it!

Tracking down wind noise

A t least when water leaks, you can see it; sound, how-ever, is invisible. It can originate in one spot but sound as if it's coming from another. If your car seems too noisy, start by finding out if a technical service bulletin (p.175) concerning wind noise has been issued for the car. If so, it's the dealer's problem to fix. If not, though, try the following.

✔Use some duct tape to seal a suspected air leak temporarily; then drive the car to see if that worked. Look particularly at joints between materials or panels—the joint at the top of the door, for instance. Look for water stain clues around the window and frame, if water can get past this seal, so can the wind. Air can sneak under windshield mold-ings, body trim, outside mirrors, and any other part that deflects air, particularly protruding sun/moon roof escutcheons. Look for an open body seam, especially around the front or bot-tom of the door frames; air can squirm up and around the door frame, then leak out the top. Once you find the air leak, plug it with auto body sealant (sometimes called body seam sealer).

✔Look closely at all weather-strips for cracks and splits. Place a dollar bill between the glass and the rubber, then close the door. The bill should be tight, but not so tight you can't pull it out.

✔Stop the engine, turn on the heater (or the air conditioner), and set the fan on *High*. Close all windows and doors. Working on the outside of the vehicle, hold one end of a short vacuum clean-er hose to your ear and move the other end over any suspected leak location. The spot where the rushing air is amplified is the spot causing the wind noise. Doctor, the patient is ready; you may now operate (and take that vacuum cleaner out of your ear!).

Chapter 10

Windows, Wipers, and Mirrors

The world is a big, big place. And to see all of it, whether you're looking forward or back, you'll have to pay attention to the glass, mirrors, and wipers. Keeping them clean and in good working order pays big dividends when it comes to safety, too. After all, you won't be able to avoid that oncoming truck if you can't see it.

But getting a good look at the view and the other drivers is only part of the story in this chapter, because you'll also have to keep the weather from getting inside. Doors and windows that seal tight keep the water out and provide the first line of defense when it comes to sealing out road noise, too. Noise reduction may not seem all that important, but you'd be surprised at the comfort difference between driving a quiet car and a rattletrap (you might even be able to hear the radio again!). Just about everything in this chapter is no-fuss, no-muss, basic do-it-yourself stuff.

Looking out

Seeing clearly

A clean windshield is more than a convenience—it can make driving a safer proposition. That's because a clean windshield won't fog up as quickly or completely as a dirty one, and it lets you see better at night too. Always clean both sides of the glass, and don't forget to clean your headlights whenever you do the windshield!

Good glass cleaners. Normal household glass cleaners work, but they're messy. These watery liquids run and drip off the glass before you get a chance to do any scrubbing. You're better off using aerosol-type automotive glass cleaners. The foam stays in place and also tends to do a better cleaning job. Most auto parts stores carry one or more brands.

Use metal polish. If the inside of your windshield is covered by a film from cigarette smoke, use Brasso metal polish (widely sold at grocery or hardware stores) to

Foam stays put

clean the glass. It won't leave scratches and is much cheaper than the special "film-cutting" automotive glass cleaners. Remove the Brasso residue with an automotive glass cleaner or windshield washer solvent.

Paper choices. The basic paper towel is barely adequate; better are those thick, reusable paper towels you can get at auto parts places. Better still, if you consider cost and availability, is crumpled-up newspaper. It cleans and dries the glass just fine and doesn't leave streaks.

In the know

In case of the vapors

A ll the plastic and vinyl in newer vehicles, as well as in stain-resistant upholstery treatments, gives off vapors. It's called "off-gassing," and the vapors usually go away on their own. As they do, though, they leave a greasy film on the inside of the glass. The result is a hazy coating that makes it tough to see through the windshield when the sun shines in. Here's how to remove the haze and encourage the departure of the vapors:

1. Wash the windows with a mixture of ½ cup of ammonia and 1 gallon of cold water.

2. Attack the vapor source. Make a sudsy solution from 2 table-spoons of dishwashing detergent and 2 quarts of warm water.

3. Wash all the plastic and vinyl surfaces, and dry them with cloth towels. Leave the windows open until the dampness is gone.

If the haze reappears, repeat the process. And if that still doesn't help, there's one other (remote) possibility. Maybe there's a tiny leak in the heater core, allowing **coolant** residue to end up on the inside of the windshield; see page 61 for more about heaters.

The garage solution. A windshield sponge/squeegee combination like the ones you see at gas stations is cheap and very handy. Keep one in a bucket filled with windshield washer solution in a safe place in your garage. That way you can wash the windows and the headlights as often as necessary between fill-ups.

Windshield leak-stopper

Getting water inside the car whenever it rains? Besides being annoying, interior leaks, especially those in the windshield area, can lead to electrical problems if the water gets to the wiring tucked into the dash. The rhythmical dripping onto your clothing can be a major distraction to safe driving, too.

Stop windshield leaks by applying clear silicone sealer (available at any auto parts store) under both edges of the rubber windshield gasket. Use a screw-

Water leak

driver to pry up the lip of the gasket, and work the sealer's spout under the rubber; then slide it along the glass as you squeeze the sealer into place. If your vehicle has a bonded windshield, with no rubber gasket, carefully apply a small bead of sealer under both edges of the windshield trim. Once dry, any excess sealer can be removed with a single-edge razor blade.

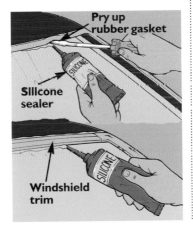

Pry up rubber gasket

Silicone sealer

Windshield trim

Rub out windshield scratches

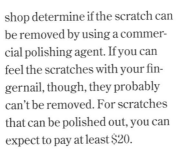

A scratch in the windshield caused by a defective wiper blade or other object can create an annoying reflection from the sun's rays. If the scratch isn't too deep, there may be a way to get rid of it without replacing the entire windshield.

✔ Try rubbing out the scratch with jeweler's rouge—you can buy it in a jewelry store or glass shop. Put a little on a cloth and rub it repeatedly over the scratch; then wash off the residue. This should take care of it.

✔ Have someone at an auto glass

shop determine if the scratch can be removed by using a commercial polishing agent. If you can feel the scratches with your fingernail, though, they probably can't be removed. For scratches that can be polished out, you can expect to pay at least $20.

✔ Many glass shops can repair stone chips in the windshield as long as they're smaller than a quarter, have no jagged edges, and are not right in front of the driver. The cost is usually between $50 and $150.

 **Quick tip**

Clean swipe

Clean your foggy car windows fast with a clean felt chalkboard eraser—keep one in the car. It works better than your handkerchief and it's faster than waiting for the defroster.

Looking out

Maintaining weatherstripping

Do squeaks erupt from your car doors every time you hit a bump? Does rain run down the *inside* of the glass? Maybe the **weatherstripping** around each door and window needs a bit of at-

Worn, dry weatherstrip

tention. If that's the problem, the fix is quick and easy as long as the weatherstripping (also called the gasket) is still intact.

Open each door and check the weatherstripping and its mating rubber surface on the door frame. If either one has small tears or cuts, you can patch them with weatherstrip adhesive or replace them. (The adhesive is

mighty sticky; remove it immediately from paint and trim using a solvent-based liquid cleaner.) If the weatherstripping is intact, you can easily revitalize it. If large sections are missing or torn, though, the entire gasket should be replaced. If it can't easily be removed, or if trim panels and moldings have to be taken off, this might be a job for a pro.

Cleaner

Weatherstripping usually sits in a channel or has small retaining clips that secure it to the door or window frame. If the clips are missing or broken, or if the weath-

erstripping keeps popping out of its channel, use a few drops of weatherstrip adhesive to hold it in place. To keep weatherstripping in top shape, here's what to do.

1. Clean the weatherstripping with a soft cloth dampened with an all-purpose household spray cleaner. Glass cleaner will work fine, too. Wipe off any cleaner residue and make sure both surfaces are completely dry.

2. Wipe or spray the weatherstripping with a product such as ArmorAll or a clear silicone paste (use paste sparingly, though!). If the product comes in an aerosol can, spray it first onto a clean cloth (some propellants will dry

Vinyl/rubber renewer

out weatherstripping). Apply it until the rubber looks slightly wet. Repeat the application if the weatherstripping is old and very dry. Periodic maintenance will keep weatherstripping healthy, soft, and flexible.

Quick tip
A blinding dash

Are the sun's rays reflecting back from the windshield into your eyes and bothering the heck out of you? Well, stop cleaning the dashboard with wax or a cleaner/protectant that contains silicone. Use warm soapy water instead.

Repairing weatherstripping

Look closely at the **weatherstripping** where the doors, hatchback, or convertible top meets the door frames and glass. Many of these hollow rubber pieces lose their shape over time and no longer seal, You may be able to restore their original shape inexpensively. The only other option is to have new weatherstripping installed.

1. If the weatherstripping has collapsed (see below), measure the length of the damage, then carefully slice the rubber at one point. Measure the inside diameter of the material and buy a length of foam backer rod to fit; ask for it at a well-stocked hardware store or home center.

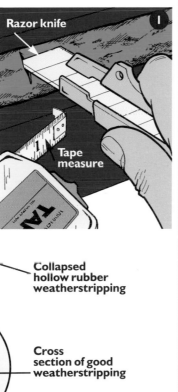

Razor knife

Tape measure

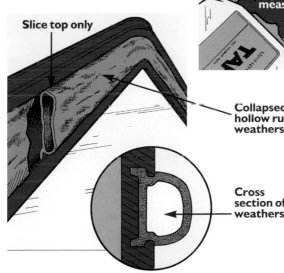

Slice top only

Collapsed hollow rubber weatherstripping

Cross section of good weatherstripping

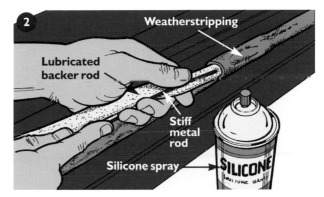

Weatherstripping

Lubricated backer rod

Stiff metal rod

Silicone spray

SILICONE

2. Lubricate the foam backer rod with aerosol silicone and slide it into the opening you made with the utility knife. Use a straightened coat hanger or metal rod to push it all the way to the end. You may have to do this in sections in order to get around bends and corners.

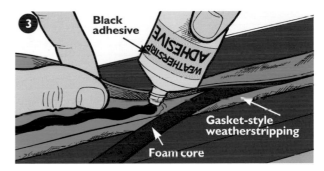

Black adhesive

WEATHERSTRIP ADHESIVE

Gasket-style weatherstripping

Foam core

3. This technique can also work on folded-over weatherstripping. If the backer rod isn't black, spray-paint it first. Then use black weatherstrip adhesive to glue it to the middle of the folded-over gasket, restoring it to its original dimension.

Wipers and such

Solving windshield wiper problems

The swoosh-swoosh of a windshield wiper doing its job is a reassuring sound. However, the rubber squeegees that touch the glass are fragile and wear out rapidly. Replacing squeegees (also called refills, inserts, or blades) every 6 months is a must-do, especially before the onset of wet weather. Usually you can purchase just the inserts, but if your car does require the complete assembly, buy a replacement version (from the auto parts store) that will allow insert-only replacement thereafter.

Even new squeegees won't guarantee perfect wiper action, so here are some common wiper problems and their cures.

Replace squeegees every 6 months for the best view.

Smearing in only one direction is common when it's very cold out, or if the squeegees are hardened from old age and can't conform to the windshield's curves. You can't change the weather, but if they're old, replace them. If you just installed new squeegees and still have this problem, you may have purchased the wrong size.

Chattering may be caused by a bent wiper arm (facing page) or, when it's *very* cold out, frozen blades. Usually the problem is caused by buildup of grease, wax, oil, or slick grime that prevents the blades from slicing the water

away. Clean the windshield with a good-quality glass cleaner or Bon Ami. The glass itself will tip you off when it's clean: Water won't bead—it will form a sheet over the surface. If the residue is thick, more than one cleaning will be

necessary. After cleaning the glass, saturate a cloth with full-strength windshield washer solution and wipe the blades down. Then flush them with plenty of water and turn on the wipers.

Water beads on the glass that won't wipe away are common where air pollution is a problem. Try increasingly strong cleaning solvents on the windshield, including perhaps a wax remover,

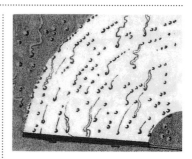

but be careful of the car's paint. If this is a recurring problem, consider buying a car cover for use when the vehicle is parked outdoors.

Smearing is caused by worn blades, a dirty windshield or wiper, or an incorrect mixture of cleaner/solvent. See if cleaning the windshield and wipers, and replacing the washer fluid, will work before replacing the blades.

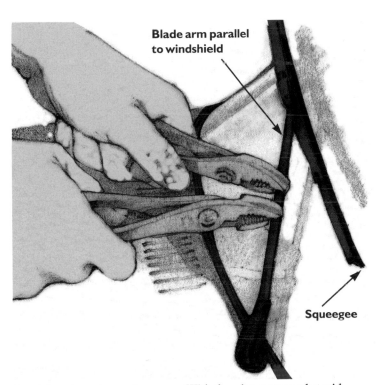

Blade arm parallel to windshield

Squeegee

Straightening a bent wiper arm. With the wipers stopped at mid-stroke, examine the blade assembly and blades. The blade arms should be parallel to the windshield, and the blades should be making full contact with the glass. If an arm is bent, use two pliers as shown to carefully twist it until the arm is parallel to the glass. If the tip of the arm is bent, remove the blade assembly before straightening the tip.

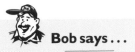

Bob says . . .

The wipers stop here

Just because the windshield wipers come to rest at different spots when you turn them off, it doesn't always mean the wiper motor has to be replaced (good thing, too, because that's a very expensive repair). A faulty motor is particularly unlikely if you can push the blades down into their correct parking position.

There's a "park switch" on the wiper motor that helps to position the wipers when they stop. If this switch is faulty, it can be replaced independently of the motor—for a lot less. Even if the problem *is* with the motor, there are alternatives to spending several hundred dollars for a new one. The cheapest option is to simply live with the condition; just push down the blades by hand if you can. Or call local auto salvage yards to find a used windshield wiper motor; it'll cost about half the price of a new one, and most will come with a replacement guarantee.

At the very least, listen closely to your mechanic before letting him junk the motor. If he says, "The contact points or brushes in the motor are sticking," yep, it's new motor time. "Looks like a bad pulse board or timer module" is also expensive news, but these parts don't come installed on a new motor—they're replaced separately (and can sometimes be found on a salvage-yard motor). If he says, "*Maybe* it's the motor; I'll replace it," ask him to test each component first to pinpoint the problem. Why spend money to replace stuff that isn't faulty?

Wipers and such

Windshield washer repairs

It's easy to forget about your windshield washer system—until it stops working. Fortunately, these systems are usually very easy to fix. If you've already checked the obvious (is there fluid in the tank?), dig a little deeper.

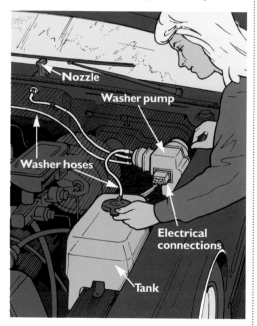

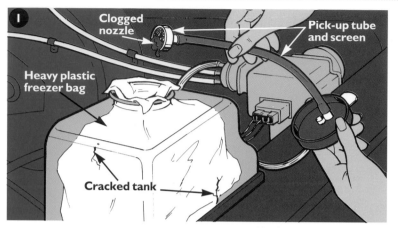

1. Take off the tank cap and check the screen on the end of the pick-up tube; maybe it's choked with grime or the tube itself is split. If the tank leaks, replace it with a new one or buy a salvaged one at a junkyard. Here's another trick: put a plastic freezer bag inside the old tank. It will hold the windshield washer fluid so all the tank has to do is hold the bag in place.

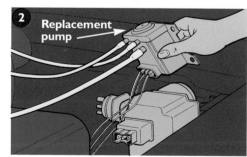

2. If the problem isn't at the tank end, it may be the washer pump (it can be on the wiper motor or inside the washer fluid tank). With the ignition on but the engine not running, listen for the pump as you or a helper operates the washer. If the pump is silent, check its electrical connections to make sure they're tight and free of corrosion. If they're OK, replace the pump with a new one. You can buy a factory replacement that will fit exactly or a universal model that may require some prep.

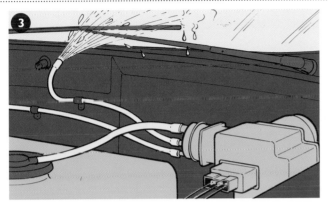

3. If the pump works, disconnect the hoses from the nozzles aimed at the windshield. Try the washer again. If fluid squirts through the hoses, wax or dirt may be clogging the nozzles (see the next step). But if no fluid came out, then the hoses are blocked either between the tank and the pump or between the pump and the nozzles. It's usually easiest to just replace loose-fitting, cracked, or clogged hoses.

4. Clogged nozzles can often be cleared with a pin, needle, or fine wire. Work carefully so you won't enlarge the nozzle accidentally. You can also flush it clean with a blast of spray lubricant.

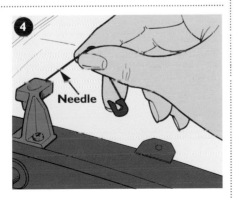

Needle

Adjusting windshield sprays

When you turn on your windshield washers and end up washing the roof instead, it's time to adjust the spray nozzles. It's easy work, but be gentle and take your time. Here's how:

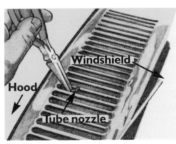

Windshield

Hood

Tube nozzle

Tube nozzles are the easiest to adjust. The tube is located just in front of the windshield or just behind the hood. Gently bend the tube with needle-nose pliers. Don't squeeze too hard or you'll crimp the tube shut!

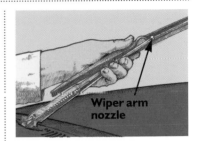

Wiper arm nozzle

Wiper arm nozzles aren't usually adjustable. Let a mechanic fix them if he can, or replace the whole assembly if he can't.

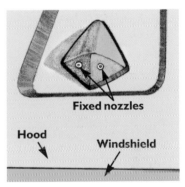

Fixed nozzles

Hood

Windshield

Fixed nozzles, while technically nonadjustable, can often be unscrewed. Slip a small piece of metal shim stock or a thin piece of plastic under them to adjust the spray direction.

Looking back

Replacing an outside mirror

Broken or cracked outside mirrors make driving very hazardous. But if you've put off replacing that damaged mirror because of cost or time considerations, it's time for a little rethinking: Repairs on a manually controlled mirror are quick, and they're inexpensive too. Electrically controlled mirrors are somewhat more complicated, however, and should be serviced by a professional.

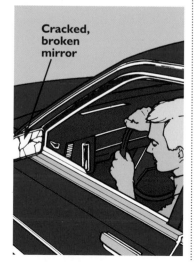

Cracked, broken mirror

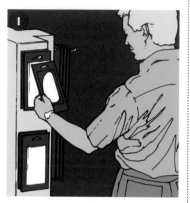

1. It's the housing that creates all the expense and hassle. But if you pay a visit to a large auto parts store, you can probably find one of several sizes/styles of replacement mirrors — just the mirror, not the housing in which it fits. Buying just the self-adhesive mirror is inexpensive and simple. In most cases it's the only thing that's needed anyhow.

2. If the original mirror is cracked but otherwise intact (no missing pieces), carefully clean the glass (beware of razor-sharp edges!), and then apply the two-sided adhesive tape supplied with the new mirror; the new mirror can go right over the old one. If pieces of the original mirror are missing, however, put on safety glasses and gloves and carefully pry or chip off the rest of the glass and remove any old adhesive. Then attach the adhesive tape to the old mirror's mounting plate. For some extra grip insurance, place a few dabs of clear silicone caulk next to the tape.

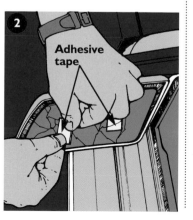

Adhesive tape

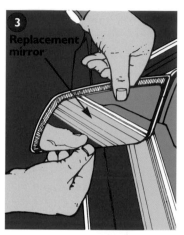

Replacement mirror

3. Align the replacement mirror with the housing, and firmly press it in place. Hold it there for about a minute to ensure that the adhesive tape grabs hold. (Make sure you don't attempt this project on a cold winter day—the adhesive may not be effective and you'll just end up with another broken mirror.)

Replacing a rearview mirror

If your rearview mirror lands in your lap, find the nearest auto parts store and buy a rearview mirror adhesive kit—it costs only a few bucks. Though you may have heard of other ways to reattach the mirror to the windshield, this one is foolproof.

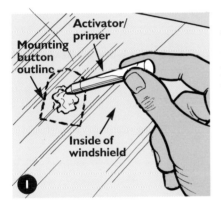

1. Mark the mounting location on the outside of the windshield with a grease pencil or a piece of masking tape. Then thoroughly scrape off any old adhesive from the windshield and the mirror's mounting button before applying the activator/primer. Let it dry for 5 minutes before using the adhesive.

2. Squeeze just 1 drop of the adhesive onto the back of the mounting button. Be sure you get the adhesive on the *back* side of the button (it's easy to get confused).

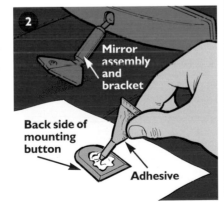

3. Press the mounting button onto the windshield and hold it in place for about a minute. Wait at least 15 minutes for the adhesive to set before mounting the mirror.

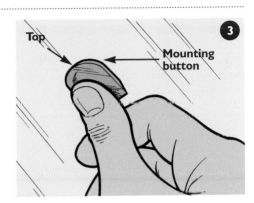

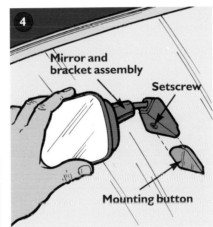

4. Slide the mirror and bracket assembly over the button; then turn the setscrew to hold the assembly in place. If by chance you glued the button on upside down or backwards, just soften the adhesive with a heat gun (low temp setting) or a hair dryer and start over again.

If it's just the mirror that's broken and the button is still in place, you can buy a new mirror and bracket assembly at your auto parts store and install it on the old mounting button. Just loosen the setscrew, slide the old assembly off, and put the new one on. Mounting buttons are the same on nearly all vehicles, whether domestic or imported.

Hauling Stuff

No matter what kind of car you drive, it does more than just get you back and forth to work. Whether you're planning an expedition to the grocery store or a Saturday morning home-center jaunt for those ever-popular plywood sheets, your car will end up hauling stuff. Can't cram it all inside? Here's a hint: there's more use for a roof than just keeping the rain off your radio.

Anyone who has wrestled with a car-top lumber load knows it's knot funny (and probably not knot-safe). In this chapter you'll learn how to do it right. And if you haul really big stuff, you'll find out how to solve a common trailer problem. You say you have lumber delivered, don't own a boat, and haven't even been in a supermarket since they stopped giving stamps? No problem—you'll learn how to tie some nifty knots that will make you the absolute hit of your next party.

Packing it

Packing to beat the wind

Today lots of cars have a roof- or trunk-mounted luggage rack. However, most of the time these racks are loaded dead wrong. When you consider that an empty rack alone can cause a 10% (or more) drop in gas mileage (deduct another mile per gallon if there's a roof rack deflector that directs air over the back window), the effects of improper packing just make a bad situation worse. Always load racks with the largest objects to the rear and the smallest things in the front. Here's how to load racks right:

Spread a tarp over the rack first. Wrap the excess over and around the luggage and secure it with octopus-style elastic cords. You'll get weather protection and a more streamlined load.

All luggage racks have load ratings. Be sure your rack can hold what you have to haul!

Best: Objects in streamlined, enclosed rooftop carrier

Good: Largest objects in rear; fairly streamlined

Worst: Largest objects are in front; most air resistance

Tie-down savvy

There are three kinds of tie-downs that are good to use with a roof rack: rubber tie-downs with hooks at each end; flat nylon straps with buckles or ratchets; and rope. All of these are available at almost any home center or hardware store.

Elastic tie-downs: The best kind for lumber are the heavy-duty black rubber straps rather than the lighter and thinner multicolored tie-downs; the rubber grips wood better. Four 2-foot and two 3-foot rubber straps should take care of most of your needs. Don't rely exclusively on rubber straps, though, because they will allow your load to move. And don't stretch straps too hard—if one snaps it could launch a dangerous projectile at you.

Flat nylon straps: The key to user-friendly nylon straps is the buckle. Buy only the kind that is self-cinching—that is, you thread the strap through the buckle, pull it tight, and it stays tight by means of a small cam-lever gripper with a thumb-operated release mechanism. Self-cinching straps can be expensive, but a good set will make you happy for life. You can also get heavy-duty ratcheting tie-down flat straps. They're made of heavier material and have S-hooks at each end, allowing you to bind a load down really tight.

Rope: This is the original all-purpose tie-down material. For large items, like full sheets of plywood, it's the only thing that works. Use a good-quality ¼-inch hemp rope. Nylon or plastic rope is slippery and stiff. Knots in the coarse-textured hemp hold better, yet are easier to untie. Take a couple of minutes to learn at least one good knot (see p.170). A length of rope about 40 feet long will allow you to hold down everything from a roof-load of plywood to bundles of trim. Keep a shorter length in the trunk, too, just for smaller loads.

Tie-down safety

Flying objects broken loose from a car roof can kill people—and have. Follow these basic safety rules:

✔ Make sure both roof racks are secure. Give them a serious yank up, forward, backward, and sideways before loading.

✔ Any load must not only be tied down but also secured against sliding sideways and forward.

✔ Slide long slender pieces of lumber, like trim, through a back window and rest them alongside the front seat. Never slide lumber in a front window, with the lumber facing forward, or you'll have a deadly spear looking for a target. Anything extending more than a foot beyond your rear bumper should have a 12x12-inch red flag on it.

✔ Drive slowly; avoid sudden stops and quick turns. Take a slow-moving route home. Check the load after the first 5 minutes of your trip to make sure that motion or wind stress hasn't loosened knots or tie-downs.

Raves about roof racks

Really good racks can cost plenty; inexpensive ones cost less than $50. Expensive racks snap on and off in about 10 seconds—no straps, no frustration—but you can't readily change them from one vehicle to another. Inexpensive racks are held in place with straps that you have to fiddle with and adjust every time you mount them.

Roof racks of any type have weight limitations, ranging from 150 to 200 pounds. That's about eighteen 8-foot 2x4's, or three sheets of ¾-inch plywood. Try to balance large loads evenly across the racks. Don't overload; too much weight will dent the roof. If you plan to carry heavy loads, buy a roof rack that has bases, or feet (the part that fits against the roof), with a broad footprint to spread the weight around.

Packing it

Hauling lumber home

You've probably spent many a Saturday morning driving back from the home center in fear of arriving with only half of your rooftop lumber load left. If you've ever felt that your loading lacked a little something on the safety side, or even if it just takes you forever to tie things down, keep reading.

Before you head out, consider the alternatives. Can you have this stuff delivered? If you have a sizable load to haul, maybe you can borrow a pickup or rent a van for the day, or make two trips.

If you do decide to carry lumber on your car roof, invest in a good-quality rack. Always load lumber with the widest pieces at the bottom, and keep ends and edges aligned. Center the load on the rack if it's larger than shown in these steps.

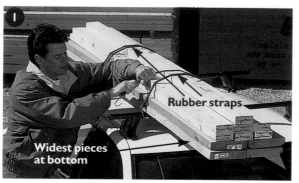

1. Tie down a load with rubber straps. Loop them under the racks on the far side, then hook both ends on the near side. Don't let a hook snap loose and put your eye out.

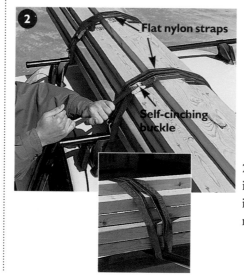

3. Prevent slide-out of individual pieces by threading and wrapping a rubber strap around internal boards within the load.

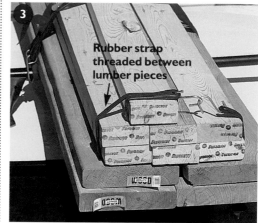

2. Secure the lumber using flat nylon straps with self-cinching buckles. The rubber straps mostly prevent movement of individual pieces; the nylon straps keep the entire load from moving around up there.

1. If you have plywood to haul, secure parallel 2x4's to the racks to serve as support rails. Use small tie-down cords. Without these support rails, it's nearly impossible to safely tie down a full 4x8-foot sheet.

2. Carry a sheet upright to within a foot of the car, with hands centered on the long edges. Rest the lower edge on your thigh, then rest the top edge on the ends of the racks and slide the sheet into place. If it's windy, get help. Tie sheets down front to back with ¼-inch rope.

Towing it

Troubleshooting trailer wiring

Trailers don't get much respect. They're pulled, pushed, and dunked under water. If your trailer lights don't work, check the ground connections first. The trailer's electrical connector should have a ground wire that goes from the connector to a ring terminal that's bolted firmly to an unpainted metal portion of the trailer. If there's no ring terminal, add one. Don't rely on the trailer ball for an electrical ground because it doesn't always provide a good electrical connection.

With wiring and politics, good connections are crucial. Wherever there's a splice, make it permanent. For really bulletproof splices, use crimped, plastic-covered butt connectors sealed with heat-shrink tubing; you can get them at a hardware store. To weatherproof flat four-pole in-line connectors when they're not in use, buy another inexpensive connector kit with male and female connectors and use them as protective caps.

 **Quick tip**
Trailer-wire holder

Tired of that trailer wiring harness hanging down behind your vehicle? Cut a slot on one end of a magnetic key storage box, just large enough for the wires to pass through, and tape the cut edges. Place the connector in the box; then stick the box on the hitch bar or on any other horizontal steel surface.

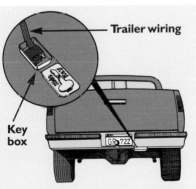

Tying it

How to use knots

A good knot can solve a lot of problems. Got a load of lumber to haul home? A trucker's hitch will cinch it down tight as can be. Need to bundle up some odd-shaped stuff? A constrictor will do the job easily (and that's no boa). In fact, you can find a knot for just about any task.

Here are some of the most useful and reliable everyday knots. Now, tying knots is a lot like playing the piano—you've got to practice, practice, practice, but once you've learned it you'll never forget. You might not spend many evenings entertaining friends with your new skills, but a good knot can make your life a lot less frustrating.

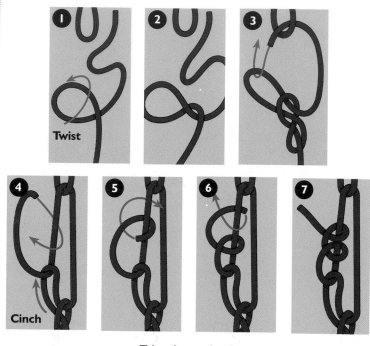

Tying down a load

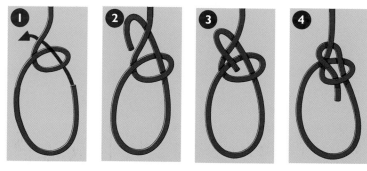

Securing anything

Bowline. Here's a do-all knot for a secure hold. The bowline is really good for stiff or thick material. A knot with nautical origins, it's simple to tie and untie, even when it's been soaked, yet it's very secure—that's why sailors have used it for thousands of years. The trucker's hitch starts with a bowline. (A sailor's pronunciation, by the way, is "bo-lyn.")

Trucker's hitch. It's rather more complex than the other knots shown here, but the trucker's hitch is highly useful for the DIYer. This is the knot you turn to when you have to tighten down that load of lumber and drywall on your trailer so you can get it home from the lumberyard. A combination of knots, the trucker's hitch begins with a bowline on one end and finishes with two half hitches (the load-tightening actually happens in step #4). This one takes practice, but its ability to cinch down a load with a ratchet-like action makes it well worth the learning time.

Cinch tight

Lengthening a rope

Sheet bend. Any time you have two short pieces of rope (or string, cable, spaghetti, whatever) and you need a longer piece, the basic sheet bend is the knot of choice. This simple knot is strong and secure as long as you keep it under tension.

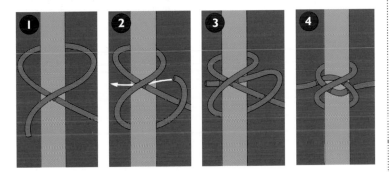

Tying up small bundles

Constrictor. This is a quick and easy knot for cinching bundles of stuff or closing trash bags. Use it any place where you need a tight, hard-to-remove knot that won't loosen.

A pair of pickup stay-puts

Here are a couple of great hold-it-in-place ideas that will work equally well in the bed of your pickup or the back of your van. Remember that cargo is most likely to move as a result of stopping, not starting. That's true of roof loads too, by the way.

Simple cargo rack. Use either 1x3's or 2x4's, depending on how much weight you'll need to restrain. Screw the four pieces together to fit just inside the wheel wells; the "ears" of the rack extend ahead of and behind the wells. Toolboxes, sandbags, and other low items will stay within the grid.

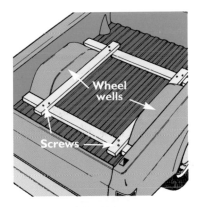

Wheel wells

Screws

Like a rod. Tired of tall things sliding all over the bed of your pickup truck as you drive? Use an adjustable shower curtain rod to keep things in their place. Just twist the rod to the proper length and it will stay in position where you put it. Use two for even greater control.

Toolbox

Adjustable shower curtain rod

Finding Parts, Information, and a Good Mechanic

he hardest thing to tuck into your
toolbox is also the most important:
good-quality information. In fact, one of
the reasons you're reading this book is
that you want hard answers to hard questions,
along with facts that will simplify the job of owning
a vehicle and save you money to boot. Well, you've
come to the right place.

In the previous chapters we've explained how to
cope with all the mechanical stuff; now it's time to
cover the consumer issues. In the following pages
you'll learn about lemon laws, extended warranties, trade-ins, low-cost parts, the mystical bulletins that manufacturers issue to dealership mechanics . . . there's even a language guide to help
you speak Mechanic so your automotive problems
will get fixed right the first time.

Visiting the mechanic

Understanding a mechanic

You won't find a bilingual Mechanic-to-English phrase book in your local library. Here, then, are some translations of common mechanic-speak. Along with the glossary on page 182, this ought to help you hold your own with any slinger of lingo.

When mechanics say: "A caliper's stuck, the pads are down to the metal, a wheel cylinder is frozen, and the lines need bleeding."
They mean: Your brakes are totally shot. A stuck **caliper** and frozen **wheel cylinder** mean these parts are rusted to the point where they no longer work. A **brake pad** that's down to the metal no longer has any friction material left, and you've probably also scored the **brake drum** or **brake rotors**. Bleeding the lines refers to removing trapped air and the old, contaminated brake fluid. Get a second opinion because this job is going to be an expensive one.

When mechanics say: "The rotors have too much run-out."
They mean: The brake rotors or discs are warped or distorted. As they wobble, they push the brake pads back; you'll feel a pulsation or vibration in the brake pedal.

When mechanics say: "The tranny's shot. The clutches are toast and the planetary's chewed up."
They mean: Get out your check-book—you've got big trouble in your automatic **transmission**. The multi-disc **clutch** packs that engage each gear are worn out, and debris from the clutches has probably damaged the planetary gearset—the mechanical drive system in the transmission. Better get a second opinion.

When mechanics say: "That noise could be a rod or main knock, piston slap, or a bad lifter."
They mean: Your engine is making expensive noises. The most serious, a rod or main bearing knock, could mean badly worn bearings, and bearing failure almost always destroys an engine. Piston slap comes from wear to a piston and causes the piston's side to slap against the **cylinder** wall—annoying but not a huge problem. A bad lifter means one of the hydraulic valve lifters is either worn or has a restricted flow of oil inside it. Annoying.

When mechanics say: "The O_2 sensor's bad, and the ECM has dropped out of closed loop and is running in the limp-home mode."
They mean: There's a problem with your vehicle's **electronic control module**. The **oxygen sensor** is no longer monitoring the air/fuel ratio being burned. The computer goes into "limp-home mode," indicating that your engine isn't running great, but it's running. The "Check Engine" light on your dash should be on.

When mechanics say: "The toe's off, it's got too much camber and it needs more caster."
They mean: You don't need a podiatrist—your car needs its front wheels aligned. "Toe" describes where each front wheel is pointed down the road. "Camber" is the in- or out-tilt of the top of the front tire, and "caster" refers to the fore-aft angle of various suspension components. If any of these is significantly out of alignment, you'll get rapid tire wear and your vehicle may pull to one side.

When mechanics say: "The engine's dropped a cylinder."
They mean: Don't look under the car—they're referring to a consistent misfire from one cylinder that is no longer doing its share of the work. The cause can be a valve, cam, piston ring, cylinder wall problem, or a spark/ignition problem.

When mechanics say: "The engine's missing."
They mean: Your engine is still under the hood. Unfortunately, one or more cylinders isn't working at all.

When mechanics say: "The warp drive's goin'—I dunna think I kin hold 'er anymore, Cap'n!"
They mean: You're at the wrong garage; beam out at once!

When a mechanic slings lingo, you'll pay for whatever you don't understand . . .

When a dealer says "No!"

Maybe you've seen it in a magazine or newspaper: A manufacturer's **technical service bulletin** (TSB) that describes the same problem your vehicle is experiencing. At your request, the dealer should check with the manufacturer to see if the TSB applies to your vehicle. If, however, he offhandedly refuses to consider your request, take your business elsewhere. You don't have to patronize a dealer just because you bought the vehicle there, even if the car is still covered under a warranty. Remember that it's the manufacturer who warrants the car, anyway, not the dealer, so what does he have to lose by checking?

But what if you have to deal with the only dealer in town and he's an ornery cuss? Well, you have to play hardball, that's what. Tell him that unless he cooperates, you'll take the matter up with the manufacturer's customer relations department or with its regional field office; contact information is in your owner's manual. If company officials fail to act, you can bring the matter to an arbitration board—the procedure is outlined in the owner's manual. Remember, though, that even if a TSB covers a problem your vehicle is having, it doesn't mean repairs are free.

Finding parts

Crash parts quality

The exterior sheet metal and plastic parts that get banged up in a crash are referred to in the industry as "crash parts," and they're big business. Vehicle manufacturers naturally want any replacement parts to come from their factories. Insurance companies, though, go for the lowest-cost parts. That's where imitation ("copycat") crash parts come in.

Imitation crash parts are usually imported from Asia, and there's a good bit of debate about their quality. Vehicle manufacturers describe quality problems in fit, finish, structural integrity, and corrosion resistance. That's why they won't cover these parts under new-vehicle warranties. Mechanics say that mounting holes and flange stampings may not line up correctly, resulting in longer installation times. Some say that the lines of an imitation panel may not be as crisp as original factory replacements. The debate rages on, but it has led to genuine parts becoming much cheaper; they now cost only a little more than imitation parts.

It's your car, so take charge of the situation. Find out from the insurance company whether the repair estimate is based on using genuine or imitation parts. If

you're willing to pay the difference between an estimate based on imitation parts and the cost of genuine parts, the body shop will do what you want.

Partspourri

Prices charged for "original equipment manufactured" (OEM) parts sold by auto dealers are often 15% to 20% higher than "aftermarket" parts offered by other suppliers. What's the difference between these parts?

I Most aftermarket parts are produced to the same exacting standards as OEM parts. However, many aftermarket parts are packaged with extra mounting hardware that allows installation on any of several similar vehicles. This lowers the cost of an aftermarket part but increases the chance that it will be installed improperly.

2 If an auto manufacturer creates a new part or a kit of parts that addresses some late-breaking change in the vehicle's design, it will probably show up first at dealerships. An equivalent aftermarket part might not be available for a while.

3 Parts manufactured by reputable aftermarket manufacturers generally carry a minimum warranty of 6 months or 6,000 miles, whichever comes first. The warranty provided by OEM manufacturers is usually 12 months or 12,000 miles, and sometimes more. And if the new part goes bad under warranty, the part *and* the installation are covered if done by the dealer.

To stay competitive, most dealers have lowered their prices dramatically on parts like spark plugs, oil, filters, and batteries. Still, be ready to pay more for maintenance-type replacement parts (like **brake shoes** and disc **brake pads** and fan belts) at the dealer.

The bottom line? If reliability, accuracy, warranty, and quality are most important to you, OEM parts are what you want. If cost is more important, go for the aftermarket part.

Information

Hard-to-find parts

Owners of older vehicles are in luck. There are sources other than a junkyard for the parts required to keep your "puff" on the road. Just 'cause it's discontinued doesn't mean it's unavailable.

✔ Your best bet for hard-to-find parts for older cars, or if you're restoring a vintage automobile, is through a publication called *Hemmings Motor News*. This is the bible of auto restoration. You should be able to buy a copy on any large newsstand, but if not, write to Hemmings Motor News, P.O. Box 100, Bennington, VT 05201. Or call (802) 442-3101. A copy costs $4.95. If you don't see what you need in the classified ads, you could place an ad asking for the part you need. In Canada, buy the Vintage Vehicle Restoration Guide, (800) 668-5539, for lists of companies that sell hard-to-find parts.

✔ In the U.S. the General Motors NOS (New Old Stock) computer system can track down parts from all over the country. Other dealers may use a CD-ROM or online system with a database of part numbers going back to the early 1970's.

How to get TSB's

Because it can be really time-consuming and sometimes difficult to locate particular **technical service bulletins** (TSB's), most new car dealers won't provide copies just for the asking. But obtaining a TSB, or finding out if there's a TSB for a problem your car is having, is way easier than it's been in the past.

The best way to locate a TSB in the U.S., is by contacting the National Highway Traffic and Safety Administration (NHTSA), Technical Reference Division. Here's how to get the information:

✔ Send a written request, explaining the specific problem you want searched, to the NHTSA. Include the make, model, year, and 17-digit vehicle identification number (VIN). Get the VIN from either the title, the registration card, or the metal plate that's visible through the windshield on the driver's side. Be sure to include your name, address, and phone number; also state that you'll pay the search fee, which usually ranges from $20 to $40. You can also ask if there's a TSB for any related problems. If anything turns up, a copy of the TSB will be mailed to you.

✔ If you want all the TSB's that have been issued to date for your vehicle, you can get them on microfiche. To find out more about this service, including fees, write the Technical Reference Division, National Highway Traffic Safety Administration, NAD-52, Room 5110, 400 Seventh St. S.W., Washington, DC 20590, (202) 366-2768. Or fax your request to (202) 493-2833.

Information

What's your old car worth?

You're sitting in a new-car showroom, eyes on the latest hot wheels, uneasily aware that you're at the mercy of people not noted for charity. Finishing his mysterious calculations, the used-car appraiser informs you ever so sadly, "Yep, your trade-in is a beauty, but it's not worth much. Here's the best I can give you for it." Unless you've done your homework, you'll never know the true market value of your vehicle.

Where the prices come from. There are numerous factors that determine what a used car is worth, but perhaps the most important is the amount of interest for that vehicle at dealer auctions. Dealer-only auctions are where dealers buy and sell vehicles to one another to adjust their inventories. Auction prices (the lowest price) are referred to as "wholesale" prices. Come trade-in time, you'll likely get less than whole-sale value because the dealer

wants to make a profit if he has to wholesale your car. The retail price (the highest price) reflects what that model is selling for in your area. (Note: Both prices are averages and are based on clean cars, in good condition, with average mileage and no major mechanical problems.) Typically, the range between wholesale and retail prices is at least $1,000, and often more than $2,000. None of these prices are fixed; they can quickly rise like hot air or drop like a rock.

Location is also a major price factor. Residents of the Snow Belt lust after four-wheel drive vehicles; in sunny climes, folks go for convertibles.

Then there's the popularity factor. Volkswagen Beetles from 1979, the last year they were sold, still sell for several thousand dollars. Not a bad price for a decades-old version of a several-decades-old design!

So you see, there's no such

thing as a set price. The market is weird and full of discrepancies.

Doing your homework. When a dealer wants to know what a car is worth, he or she refers to a variety of publications such as Kelley's *Blue Book, The Canadian Red Book,* or the *Official Used Car Guide* of the National Automobile Dealers Associa-

tion (NADA). These books, along with Edmund's *Used Car Prices* (written for us average folks), can be found at most bookstores. They have a huge influence on what your trade-in offer will be; double-check to see if the offer is fair or not. Also, there are numerous used-car pricing guide software programs, plus online services that offer information on resale values. Still, judging used-car value is more of an art than a science. Have your car appraised at a couple of local used-car lots. Check the prices in the local classified ads to see what people are asking for vehicles similar to yours. Call a few of the ads to find out about mileage and condition.

Making sense of it all.
When you're done, sit down with paper and pencil and make some sense out of the different numbers. Factor in such aspects as condition (be honest), mileage (12,000 miles per year is considered the norm—more miles lowers the price). Remember that the dealer will deduct for reconditioning (the cleaning process a used car receives before it can be put on the lot). Deduct a reasonable amount for each major repair your car requires (such as tires, body work, and the like).

With these numbers in hand, you're ready to negotiate. A car in better-than-average condition with low mileage should get a top-end price, whether trade-in or retail. Of course there won't be much bargaining if your trade-in is painted pink and has a diesel engine, but if you're not happy with an offer, visit another dealer.

Bob says . . .
Be wise about warranties

If your car is under warranty, let the dealer do any work. If you turn it over to a local garage, you might not be reimbursed for a repair unless the car broke down when the dealership was closed. The most you'll be reimbursed is the amount the manufacturer would have paid the dealership for the same repair.

Has your car been recalled?

A vehicle can be recalled for either a safety- or an emissions-related deficiency. (An emissions deficiency occurs when a car emits pollutants in excess of that allowed by law.)

Even if you're the first owner of the vehicle, you may have missed or perhaps ignored a recall notice. If you're the second or third owner, don't assume that the prior owners responded to recalls and had the repairs made.

At the time a recall is announced, written notices are sent to registered owners of the affected vehicles, informing them that dealers will make the repairs free of charge. The manufacturer, by producing enough replacement parts, will attempt to have their dealers correct the defect as quickly as possible.

Someone who buys a used car and wants to find out whether that car has been recalled should write down the car's 17-digit Vehicle Identification Number (VIN). The VIN is also written on the car's bill of sale and registration. Armed with this information, call the dealer.

If you don't want to bother with a dealer, you can find out if your vehicle has been recalled for a safety- or emissions-related problem. The former are overseen by the National Highway Traffic Safety Administration (NHTSA); the latter fall under the Environmental Protection Agency (EPA). For either type of problem, call the NHTSA at (800) 424-9393. When you call, you need to know the year, make, and model of the vehicle, as well as its VIN.

If you already paid for a repair and the same repair is later part of a recall, you'll be entitled to a refund. That's why keeping track of recall notices can save you thousands of dollars.

Information

Know your rights: lemon laws

Consumer protection laws, nicknamed "lemon laws," have been enacted in every state and in most provinces. Manufacturers can be forced to repair (at no cost to the owner) or replace an unusually problematic new vehicle during the first 12 months (or up to 48 months in Canada). Problems must substantially impair the use, value, or safety of the vehicle. If you've tried without success to repair such a lemon, contact the manufacturer and request a resolution under its dispute settlement program. Any decision made during this arbitration process is binding on the manufacturer but not on the owner of the car. In most provinces you can work through the Canadian Motor Vehicle Arbitration Plan, (800)207-0685.

If this fails, it may be time to initiate legal action. To support your claim, hold on to all work orders, copies of rental agreements if you had to rent a replacement car, and records of phone conversations, including who you spoke to and when. If you win, you'll still be responsible for normal wear and tear, plus mileage, on your vehicle. A suit could be costly, but it may be the only way to rid yourself of a headache.

 **Bob says . . .**

Let your computer gopher it

Home computers and online services have made it easy to locate information from virtually any vehicle manufacturer. Start with a keyword search (i.e., wheels, car, or the manufacturer's name). From there it'll be easy to find an e-mail address for the manufacturer, a forum for swapping stories and information about your vehicle, or a news group related to auto issues.

Extended warranties

When you're purchasing either a new or a used car, most dealers will want to sell you an extended warranty. Are they worth the money? Usually not. Some have so many exclusions buried in the fine print that they cover little. They are, however, high-profit sidelines for dealers.

Dealers are funny about extended warranties. While they're trying to sell you the vehicle, they brag about the great factory warranty; then as soon as you agree to buy, suddenly that factory warranty isn't adequate anymore.

If you want peace of mind, take the cost of the extended warranty and place it in a special bank account (never finance an extended warranty); use this money only for repairs not covered by the standard warranty.

Overall, warranties are a snake pit of conflicting and confusing financial concerns. They may sound good, but the reality may not be so wonderful. The bottom line: Most financial consultants and consumer groups consider extended warranties a poor choice.

Other warranties

In accordance with U.S. federal law, emissions control system components on 1994 and older vehicles are guaranteed for anywhere from 2 years or 24,000 miles to 8 years or 80,000 miles, depending on the part. In Canada, emissions control components are warranted for up to 5 years on vehicles built since the mid-1980's. If during the warranty period an emissions control system part fails, the cost of having it installed will be paid by the manufacturer. The warranty is in effect for the original owner of the vehicle and all subsequent owners until the warranty period expires.

Another section of the emissions warranty is less clear-cut. It covers non-emissions control system components, which when they go bad result in an increase in air pollution. Depending on the manufacturer and mileage, the cost of cleaning fuel injectors, for example, may be covered; but only if an emission problem is the reason for the repair.

The emissions warranty situation has a lot of people confused. Basically, every vehicle owner should study the emission warranty that came with his or her vehicle and be aware of its general provisions. If a dispute arises between you and the dealer over whether a repair is or isn't covered, remember that it's up to the manufacturer, not the dealer, to make that decision.

If your vehicle fails a state-mandated emissions check during the emission warranty period, the cost of repairs should be borne by the manufacturer.

A reference card for your vehicle

If you do your own auto maintenance, you can simplify things when you shop for parts and supplies by using this wallet card. Either make a photocopy or cut it out and paste or tape it to a business card. Fill in the blanks, including your preferred brands of filters, oil, and any part numbers. Then tuck the card away in your wallet, where it'll always be on hand for quick and easy reference when shopping. No more thumbing through guides the size of phone books at the auto parts store to find the right part numbers!

Year	Make		Model	
Engine (size & number of cylinders)		Turbo?		Diesel?
Oil filter no.	Air filter no.			
Oil (brand & weight)				
VIN (vehicle identification number)				
PCV valve no.		Breather filter no.		Fuel filter no.
Spark plugs		Gap		
Tire size		Misc.		

Glossary

A

accumulator: The low side of an air-conditioning system. It removes moisture from (and stores) liquid refrigerant. *See also* **receiver dryer**.

air management valves: One-way valves that prevent exhaust gases from entering the air pump.

alternator: A device that produces alternating current (AC) for the car by spinning a magnet inside a stationary conductor. *See also* **generator**.

antifreeze: A liquid mixed with water to keep the water from freezing in the cooling system. *See also* **coolant**.

antilock brakes: A brake system that's controlled by computer to reduce wheel skid and prevent wheel lockup. It helps you to keep control of the car on a slippery surface and when braking hard in an emergency. Don't "pump" antilock brakes in a skid, as you would with standard brakes, or they'll be less effective.

Arrgh: The sound a driver makes when his or her car breaks down.

axle: A shaft that transfers power from the differential to the wheels.

B

brake booster: A device that helps to reduce braking effort.

brake caliper: A hydraulic piston assembly that holds disc brake pads.

brake drag: Drag is created when brake shoes or brake pads continually rub against a brake drum or disc. It can lead to brake failure.

brake drum: This large circular surface is what a brake shoe presses against to stop a vehicle.

brake pad: The replaceable friction material used on disc brakes.

brake pull: When a vehicle moves unexpectedly left or right as you press the brakes, that's pull. The brakes may be out of adjustment or the tires may need more air.

brake pulsation: If you can feel the brake pedal, steering wheel, or the entire car vibrate as you step on the brakes, have the brakes serviced.

brake rotor: In a vehicle with disc brakes, the rotor is the shiny metal disc that the brake pads squeeze to stop the vehicle.

brake shoe: A curved, replaceable friction material that's used on drum brakes. No longer made of asbestos.

C

caliper: *See* **brake caliper**.

camber: The inward or outward tilt of the wheel and tire assembly.

carburetor: A wondrous device found under the air filter; it mixes fuel and air and delivers them to the combustion chambers.

clutch: Driver-operated device that engages and disengages the engine from the transmission. Found only on cars with a manual transmission.

clutch disc: When pressed against the flywheel, it transfers power from the engine to the transmission.

clutch pressure plate: Holds the clutch disc against the flywheel.

clutch release fork: Device that disengages the clutch disc from the flywheel by pushing on the pressure plate release springs.

cold cranking amps: A measure of battery power; more is better.

combustion chamber: The top of the cylinder where the air/fuel mixture ignites.

constant velocity joint: A coupling that allows the drive axle to rotate at a constant speed at various angles when the car turns.

coolant: The mixture of antifreeze and water (usually 50:50) that circulates through the engine to cool it.

coolant sensor: Measures the temperature of the engine coolant.

crank sensor/cam sensor: Device that indicates the position of the crankshaft and/or the cam shaft. The ECU uses this information.

CV joint: *See* **constant velocity joint**.

cylinder: Passage inside the cylinder block that holds the pistons.

cylinder block: The part of the engine to which everything else is attached. It contains passages for lubricants and coolant, and it's really heavy.

cylinder head: Contains the intake and exhaust valves, along with passages for the air/fuel mixture to enter (and exhaust to leave) the combustion chamber.

D

differential: Gear assembly used to transfer power from the transmission to the rear axles, and thus to the rear wheels.

distributor: Transfers the voltage surge from the ignition coil to the distributor cap and the spark plug wires in the correct firing order.

dog tracking: What happens when rear brakes grab too quickly and pull the back of the car down as you stop.

DoT 3/4: U.S. Department of Transportation rating system for the boiling point, blend, and performance of brake fluid.

drive axle: The shafts that connect the transaxle to the front wheels.

driveshaft: In rear-wheel-drive cars, it connects the transmission to the differential.

drum: *See* **brake drum**.

E

ECU: *See* **electronic control unit**.

EGR valve: *See* **exhaust gas recirculation valve**.

electronic control unit (ECU): The computer "brain" of the fuel and emissions control system. It analyzes information and adjusts the operation of various components. It also turns on the "Check Engine" or "Service Engine Soon" light. Sometimes called the electronic control module (ECM).

evaporator core: The part of the air-conditioning system where refrigerant changes from a liquid to a gas and absorbs heat from the air.

exhaust gas recirculation valve: The EGR valve is part of the emissions control system; it recirculates exhaust gas into the intake manifold, cooling the combustion chamber.

exhaust manifold: Metal tubes that lead exhaust gases from the engine to the exhaust system. *See also* **intake manifold**.

F

fire extinguisher: For maximum versatility, automotive models should be rated A-B-C: A for trash, wood, and paper fires; B for liquid, solvent, and grease fires; C for electrical fires.

firewall: The wall between the engine compartment and the passenger compartment.

firing order: The order in which spark plugs fire; the sequence determines when each piston is in the exact position to begin its power stroke.

flywheel: A metal plate bolted to the crankshaft; it usually includes a gear that's engaged by the starter motor.

fuel injector: Electrically controlled valve that delivers a precise amount of pressurized fuel into each combustion chamber. Most cars have them instead of a carburetor these days.

fuel pressure regulator: A device that maintains proper fuel pressure under all driving conditions and engine loads.

fuel pump: A mechanical or electrical pump that pressurizes the fuel system to move gas from tank to engine.

fuse: A tiny electrical device that cuts current in a circuit that is overloaded or shorted to ground. This prevents damage to other components.

G

gas-charged shocks: Shock absorbers filled with a low-pressure gas to smooth a car's ride during continuous rapid up-and-down movement.

generator: Device that produces direct current (DC) by spinning a conductor inside a stationary magnet. It's the cylinder-shaped device your fan belt goes around. *See also* **alternator**.

grab: "Touchy" brakes. Slight pressure on the pedal causes the brakes to lock up. Have brakes serviced.

H

hard pedal: (1) The trip up Mt. Washington on a bicycle. (2) When extreme pressure must be placed on the brake pedal to stop the car. Have brakes serviced promptly.

head gasket: Gasket between the cylinder head and the engine block that helps to contain pressure in the cylinders.

I

IAC: *See* **idle air control**.

idle air control (IAC): Controlled by the ECU, this device regulates idle speed in fuel injected engines.

independent suspension: A suspension design that allows each wheel to move up and down independently of the others. It can be found on just two wheels or on all four.

intake manifold: Metal tubes that channel the air/fuel mixture from the carburetor into the cylinders. *See also* **exhaust manifold.**

intake valve: When opened, it allows the fuel/air mixture to enter the combustion chamber.

K

knock sensor: (1) The front door of your house. (2) A device that warns the ECU that the engine is pinging (knocking).

L

lean/rich fuel condition: A lean fuel mixture has too much air, a rich mixture has too much fuel.

load leveler springs: Helical springs that maintain normal vehicle height.

low pedal: When the brake pedal nearly touches the floor before the brakes begin to function. Bad news!

M

manifold absolute pressure (MAP) sensor: A device that detects engine load by measuring air pressure or vacuum in the intake manifold.

MAP sensor: *See* **manifold absolute pressure sensor**.

mass airflow sensor: A device that measures and straightens the flow of air entering the throttle housing.

master cylinder: A piston-type pump that produces pressure in the brake hydraulic system.

muffler: The exhaust system part that reduces noise made by an engine.

O

octane: The component of gasoline that reduces knocking. Don't use a higher-octane gas than necessary.

Glossary

oxygen (O_2) sensor: Part of the emissions control system, it measures the amount of oxygen in the exhaust.

P

PCV valve: Emission device that routes oil pan (crankcase) vapors to the intake manifold to be burned during combustion.

petcock: A small valve, either metal or plastic, at the bottom of the radiator for draining coolant.

ping: An engine noise caused by faulty fuel ignition.

positive crankcase ventilation valve: See **PCV valve.**

PSI: Pounds per square inch. A measure of pressure.

R

R-12: Environmentally hazardous refrigerant once used in most automotive air-conditioning systems.

R-134a: An environmentally safe refrigerant now used in A/C systems.

radiator: A large copper or aluminum chamber in front of the engine. Hot engine coolant that circulates through the radiator is cooled and then recirculated to the engine.

rebuild: To repair or replace any worn or defective parts of an automotive component, such as an engine.

receiver dryer: The high side of an air-conditioning system. It removes moisture from the air and stores refrigerant. *See also* **accumulator.**

refrigerant: Chemical compounds that absorb, carry, and release heat from an air-conditioning system.

remanufacture: To replace all wearing parts, gaskets, and seals and make sure all other components are within manufacturer's specifications.

road crown: A slight arch built into most roads that prevents water from collecting on the road surface.

rotor: *See* **brake rotor.**

RPM: Revolutions per minute. A measure of how fast an object (especially a shaft) is turning.

S

SAE: Society of Automotive Engineers, an automotive trade group.

severe usage: Any use that puts unusual stress or wear on a car, such as short trips, extreme temperatures, and stop-and-go traffic.

shock absorber: The part of a suspension that uses air pressure or hydraulic pressure to dampen the up-and-down motion of a vehicle. Typically found near each wheel.

strut cartridge: Replaceable shock absorber unit of MacPherson strut.

sway bar: A spring-steel rod that resists body roll during sharp turns. Part of the suspension system.

T

technical service bulletin (TSB): Information sent from the vehicle manufacturer to a dealer's service department that describes changes in a maintenance or repair procedure.

thermal vacuum valve: An emissions control part that opens or closes depending on engine temperature.

thermostat: A simple but critically important device that regulates temperature. In a cold engine, it closes to block the flow of coolant going to the radiator (thus providing faster warm-ups), then opens when the coolant reaches a specific temperature.

throttle position sensor (TPS): An emissions system device that monitors the position of the throttle plate.

toe-in: When the leading edges of a pair of wheels are closer together than the trailing edges. *See also* **toe-out.**

toe-out: When the leading edges of a pair of wheels are farther apart than the trailing edges. *See also* **toe-in.**

torque: A turning or twisting force.

torque converter: A coupling between the engine and an automatic transmission that acts like the clutch on a manual transmission. It can double the engine's torque, but can cause all sorts of pesky problems if faulty.

Torx: A six-pointed screwdriver or socket that comes in assorted sizes from T8 (smallest) to T60 (largest).

TPS: *See* **throttle position sensor.**

transaxle: In front-wheel drive cars, an assembly consisting of a transmission (manual or automatic) and a differential. Located next to the engine.

transmission: Transmits the engine's power to the differential.

TSB: *See* **technical service bulletin.**

V

vacuum port: The part of a device that a vacuum hose connects to.

viscosity: A measure of a liquid's resistance to flow. Water has low viscosity; honey has high viscosity. Typically used to describe oil's "thickness."

W

water pump: Part of the cooling system that circulates coolant through the engine, radiator, and heater core.

weatherstripping: The soft rubber that seals the doors, windows, and trunk from the weather.

wheel chock: A block of wood placed behind a tire to keep the vehicle from moving as it's being jacked up.

wheel cylinder: A piston that pushes a brake shoe against a brake drum.

Hey! What's wrong with my car?

When your vehicle gets sick, you might not know the problem but at least you can report the symptoms. Photocopy the following diagnostic worksheets, fill out the most appropriate one, and insist that it be attached to the service department's work order. If you supply good information, it will go a long way toward helping your mechanic understand, identify, and repair the problem correctly—the first time.

Hard Start / No Start

When does the problem occur? (Check all that apply)

Engine temp.

○ Cool
○ Warm
○ Hot
○ At warm-up
○ All the time
○ Other (explain) _____

Weather conditions

○ Very cold
○ Cool
○ Hot
○ Raining
○ Snow/ice

○ Cold
○ Warm
○ Dry
○ Wet roads
○ Humid

How often does it occur?
(Check all that apply)

○ Always
○ Every few min.
○ ...few hours
○ ...few days
○ ...few weeks
○ ...few months
○ Every ____ to ____ miles.

○ Just started
○ Since new
○ Variable
○ Getting better
○ Getting worse
○ I'm not sure

Symptom

○ Hard start
○ Long crank
○ No start (cranks OK)
○ Stalls after starting

Type of gas used

○ Many brands
○ Regular UL
○ Plus UL
○ Premium UL

Shifting Problems (automatic transmissions)

When does the problem occur? (Check all that apply)

Engine temp.

○ Cool
○ Warm
○ Hot
○ At warm-up
○ All the time
○ Other (explain) _____

Weather conditions

○ Very cold
○ Cool
○ Hot
○ Raining
○ Snow/ice

○ Cold
○ Warm
○ Dry
○ Wet roads
○ Humid

How often does it occur?
(Check all that apply)

○ All the time
○ Every few min.
○ ...few hours
○ ...few days
○ ...few weeks
○ ...few months
○ Every ____ to ____ miles.

○ Just started
○ Since new
○ Variable
○ Getting better
○ Getting worse
○ I'm not sure

Symptom

○ Shifts too soon/too late
○ Doesn't shift correctly
○ Overdrive doesn't work
○ Starts in "D" or "R"
○ Fluid leaking
○ Noisy
○ Will not shift
○ Engages poorly
○ Slips out of gear

Hey! What's wrong with my car?

Engine Runs Rough or Loses Power

When does the problem occur? (Check all that apply)

Engine temp.

- ○ Cool
- ○ Warm
- ○ Hot
- ○ At warm-up
- ○ All the time
- ○ Other (explain) _____

Weather conditions

- ○ Very cold
- ○ Cool
- ○ Hot
- ○ Raining
- ○ Snow/ice

- ○ Cold
- ○ Warm
- ○ Dry
- ○ Wet roads
- ○ Humid

How often does it occur?
(Check all that apply)

- ○ Always
- ○ Every few min.
- ○ ... few hours
- ○ ... few days
- ○ ... few weeks
- ○ ... few months
- ○ Every _____ to _____ miles.

- ○ Just started
- ○ Since new
- ○ Variable
- ○ Getting better
- ○ Getting worse
- ○ Unknown

Symptom

- ○ "Service Engine Soon" or other malfunction indicator light on
- ○ Rough idle
- ○ Engine misses
- ○ Engine stalls
- ○ Engine hesitates
- ○ Engine stumbles
- ○ Other (explain) _____

- ○ Idles too high
- ○ Idles too low
- ○ Exhaust smoke
- ○ Engine surges
- ○ Car jerks
- ○ Car pings/knocks

- ○ Excess oil consumption
- ○ Poor power or performance
- ○ Engine misses while driving
- ○ Sulfur/rotten egg odor
- ○ Car backfires
- ○ Engine speed changes while gas pedal is steady
- ○ Engine runs after key is turned off

Poor gas mileage

- ○ On the highway
- ○ In the city

Brakes, Steering, and Suspension

Symptom

○ Vehicle pulls right ... when?_____
○ Vehicle pulls left ... when?_____ _____
○ Steering wheel vibrates at _____ MPH
○ Excessive play in steering
○ Erratic steering while braking
○ Steering wheel slow to return after cornering

○ Suspension bottoms out
○ Car leans/sways in corners
○ Brake warning light on
○ Traction control light on
○ Uneven tire wear

○ Car sits unevenly
○ Car "dog tracks"
○ ABS light on
○ Ride is too soft

Hard to steer

○ Steering wheel off center   ○ Steering wheel too hard to turn   ○ Car wanders

Shimmy / vibration: where is it?

○ Don't know, but I can feel it
○ Floor

○ Front of car
○ Seat

○ Rear of car
○ Other: _____ _____

Brake pedal

○ Noisy   ○ Excessive travel   ○ Squeaks   ○ Hard to push   ○ Mushy   ○ Pulses

When does it occur?

○ Cold days   ○ Hot days   ○ Wet days   ○ All the time   ○ Intermittent

○ At road speed   ○ Accelerating   ○ Decelerating   ○ When I'm parking

Hey! What's wrong with my car?

Electrical and Audio Systems

Audio component affected

- ○ Only the radio
- ○ Only the tape player
- ○ Only the CD player
- ○ AM   ○ FM

- ○ Antenna
- ○ Clock
- ○ Cellular phone
- ○ FM Stereo

- ○ Audio controls on steering wheel
- ○ Equalizer

Speakers
- ○ Front   ○ Left
- ○ Rear   ○ Right

Audio system problems

- ○ Doesn't work
- ○ Controls inoperative
- ○ Other (explain) _____

- ○ Noisy
- ○ Fuse blows

- ○ Static
- ○ Poor reception

Cassette player? CD player?
- ○ Won't load   ○ Won't eject

Other electrical components

List the accessory or other items experiencing problems

What is it? _____

- ○ Doesn't work at all
- ○ Warning lamp on
- ○ Other (explain) _____

- ○ Fuse blows
- ○ Noisy

- ○ Works, but improperly
- ○ No control

- ○ Works sometimes

When does the problem occur?

- ○ Always
- ○ Intermittent
- ○ Other (explain) _____

- ○ Hot weather
- ○ After _____ minutes

- ○ Cold weather
- ○ Rough or bumpy roads

- ○ After starting
- ○ After extended use

Squeaks, Rattles, and Other Noises

Area of noise

○ Engine compartment	○ Left	○ Center	○ Right	○ Don't know
○ Front suspension	○ Left	○ Center	○ Right	○ Don't know
○ Rear suspension	○ Left	○ Center	○ Right	○ Don't know
○ Passenger compartment	○ Left	○ Center	○ Right	○ Don't know
○ Instrument panel	○ Left	○ Center	○ Right	○ Don't know

○ Trunk door or hatchback	○ Left front door	○ Right front door	○ Left rear door	○ Right rear door
○ Rear seat area	○ Console			

Noise sounds like a . . .

○ Knock	○ Metallic noise	○ Roar	○ Rattle	○ Ticking
○ Squeak	○ Scrape	○ Whine	○ Other:_____	

How often does it occur?

○ Continuous	○ Often	○ Just started	○ Since new	○ Intermittent

When does it occur?

○ All the time	○ Light acceleration	○ Braking	○ On deceleration
○ Cold days	○ Hard acceleration	○ Idling in gear	○ Only when moving
○ Hot days	○ Light bumps	○ Idling out of gear	○ At steady speeds
○ Heavy bumps	○ On turns	○ Humid or rainy	○ In reverse gear
○ At _____ MPH	○ At _____ RPM	○ Smooth pavement	

Index

Index

If you have any questions or comments, feel free to write us at:

THE FAMILY HANDYMAN
7900 International Drive
Suite 950
Minneapolis, MN 55435